I0796366

Praise for

UNLEARNING JEWISH ANXIETY

"Anxiety is no new phenomenon. . . . Denver-based rabbi Caryn Aviv put the final touch on her book manuscript for Monkfish—*Unlearning Jewish Anxiety: How to Live with More Joy and Less Suffering*—on the very day that an antisemite firebombed Jewish people in nearby Boulder."

—**CATHY LYNN GROSSMAN**, *Publishers Weekly*

"With fierce compassion and practical wisdom, Caryn Aviv's *Unlearning Jewish Anxiety* is a necessary gift for our trembling times. She names our inherited fears and invites us into the sacred work of tending our own lives so that healing might ripple outward. Again and again she reminds us: 'It's up to us' to nurture our bodies and spirits, to claim safety, worth, and belonging. This book gently re-teaches the nervous system to choose purpose over panic. Read these pages slowly, share them in community, and let them guide you toward healing. You'll be glad you did."

—**RABBI MENACHEM CREDITOR**, author of *And Yet We Love: Poems* and *Timeless Torah*

"*Unlearning Jewish Anxiety* is a radiant JEW-el in the murky stew of self-help books about managing anxiety, mindfulness and trauma healing. Rabbi Aviv offers a beautifully written, accessible guide to managing the unique habits, patterns and legacies of Jewish anxiety. Grounded in neuroscience, Jewish feminist wisdom and trustworthy ethics, she also 'walks the talk' by weaving her personal experience with managing Jewish anxiety with compelling insights from teaching these embodied practices to others. This is a powerful toolkit for friends, families, and communities to read and practice together in the spirit of transformation and healing at a time of urgency, brutality and division."

—**KAREN ERLICHMAN, DMin, LCSW**, spiritual director, psychotherapist, community facilitator

"Filled with wise teachings, interviews, and stories that help us remember who we are beneath our fear, Caryn Aviv gifts us with a guidebook (to understanding and undoing our Jewish anxiety,) in service of the better angels of our humanity. An important read that is extremely relevant for our day."

—**RABBI DR. TIRZAH FIRESTONE**, author of *Wounds into Wisdom: Healing Intergenerational Jewish Trauma*

"Caryn Aviv reminds readers that authentic and sustainable Jewish identities, communities, and practices are shaped but not defined by the worlds and identities Jewish people inhabit. *Unlearning Jewish Anxiety* invites readers to reimagine learned patterns and offers a practical toolkit for building healthy habits that keep the mind, body, and ultimately the world in good repair."

—**SHAWN LANDRES, PhD**, coeditor, *Personal Knowledge and Beyond*, and cofounder, Jumpstart Labs

"Rabbi Caryn Aviv writes with rare clarity and care, helping us transform the weight of inherited anxiety into fertile ground for awareness, creativity, and renewal. This is a deeply needed book—one that reminds us that the work of healing ourselves is also the work of healing the world."

—**RABBI ADINA ALLEN**, creative director, Jewish Studio Project

"Reading this book is like having a conversation with a sociologist, a rabbi, and good friend all in one. Caryn Aviv provides wisdom, understanding, and guidance on how to free ourselves from anxious patterns. In a gentle, conversational manner she provides teachings and practices to help unlearn inherited patterns of Jewish anxiety."

—**AMY GROSSBLATT PESSAH**, rabbi, spiritual director, author of *Parenting on a Prayer*

"Aviv weaves neuroscience with Jewish practice to show how anxiety builds and how 'kindfulness'—pausing, breathing, listening—can loosen its grip. She refuses shame and insists on our inherent safety, worth, and belonging. This beautiful book isn't a scold; it's a companion: practical tools, wise stories, and a deeply Jewish path toward more joy and less suffering."

—**RABBI SHIRA STUTMAN**, co-host of the Chutzpod! podcast, and founder of Mixed Multitudes

UNLEARNING JEWISH ANXIETY

HOW TO LIVE WITH MORE JOY AND LESS SUFFERING

CARYN AVIV

BOOK PUBLISHING COMPANY
RHINEBECK, NEW YORK

Unlearning Jewish Anxiety: How to Live with More Joy and Less Suffering © 2026 by Caryn Aviv

All rights reserved. No part of this book may be used or reproduced in any manner without the consent of the publisher, except in critical articles or reviews. Contact the publisher for information.

Paperback ISBN 9781966608110
eBook ISBN 9781966608127

Library of Congress Control Number 2025038239

Library of Congress Cataloging-in-Publication Data

Names: Caryn, Aviv author
Title: Unlearning Jewish anxiety : how to live with more joy and less suffering / Caryn Aviv.
Description: Rhinebeck, New York : Monkfish Book Publishing Company, [2026] | Includes bibliographical references.
Identifiers: LCCN 2025038239 (print) | LCCN 2025038240 (ebook) | ISBN 9781966608110 paperback | ISBN 9781966608127 ebook
Subjects: LCSH: Anxiety--Religious aspects--Judaism | Stress (Psychology)--Religious aspects--Judaism | Self-help techniques--Religious aspects--Judaism | Spiritual life--Judaism | LCGFT: Essays
Classification: LCC BM729.J4 C37 2026 (print) | LCC BM729.J4 (ebook) | DDC 296.7--dc23/eng/20251119
LC record available at https://lccn.loc.gov/2025038239
LC ebook record available at https://lccn.loc.gov/2025038240

Monkfish Book Publishing Company
22 East Market Street, Suite 304
Rhinebeck, New York 12572
(845) 876-4861
monkfishpublishing.com

In memory of my grandparents:
Bessie and Charles Abrams, Naomi and George Louis

For Sasha Meirav Drinkwater

The whole world is a very narrow bridge,
and the most important thing
is to not fear at all.
—Rabbi Nachman of Breslov

Loosen, loosen, baby
You don't have to carry
The weight of the world in your muscles and bones
Let go, let go, let go
Holy breath, and holy name
Will you ease
Will you ease this pain?
—Aly Halpert

CONTENTS

PREFACE

Dreaming of Home

We want so much to be in that place
where we are respected and cherished,
protected, acknowledged,
nurtured, encouraged, and heard.

And seen, seen
in all our loveliness,
in all our fragile strength.

And safe, safe in all our trembling
vulnerability. Where we are known
and safe, safe and known—
is it possible?

—Merle Feld[1]

All of us yearn to be safe, seen, and loved. We need recognition, and we want to belong. For Jews living in a society with deeply embedded anti-Jewish contempt, this affirmation—that we are safe and worthy, that we belong—often feels difficult to experience, let alone to trust.

We learn, from our ancestors and elders, our complicated history of oppression and violence. We learn, from living in this difficult world, that many people loathe us. Safety sometimes feels like a luxury or privilege. When our houses of prayer and community centers are targeted for violence, when we are harassed on the street or asked suspiciously about "where we come from," when the word "Zionist" is used with undisguised contempt, many of us feel profoundly unsafe.

We learn in a variety of ways that we are viewed as *conditionally* worthy, that we can belong only under certain circumstances that invite us to minimize, hide, or deny our Jewishness. For many of us, this is impossible, because of what we look like, what we choose to wear (with pride and fear), how we walk and talk, how we think, feel, and express ourselves. When we experience threats and micro-aggressions about our skin color, our hair texture, the shape of our noses, our accents, our gestures, the speed or sound of our speech, our postures, our body sizes, our wealth or lack thereof, we feel unsafe in our bodies, unloved, unworthy, and insecure about our place in the world.

Sometimes we worry about whether we truly belong in the communities where we live. This includes our own Jewish communities, where some Jews unconsciously and unkindly act as gatekeepers, telling us in myriad ways that we're not enough. When people of all ages and stages get trolled in person and online for speaking out about anti-Jewish oppression or advocating for what we think and feel about an issue as Jewish people, we sometimes feel unsafe.

Our fears for our safety, our anxieties about our inherent worth and dignity, and our questions about whether we truly belong are grounded in reality. This takes a toll on our well-being as humans and as Jews. It's exhausting. It's not our fault.

And yet. There are so many moments when we experience fear and uncertainty as Jewish habitual responses to the world, when in fact we are safe in the present moment. We habitually respond with anxiety about our worthiness when our inherent dignity is not in question. We presume exclusion when the question of whether we belong is not at stake. We constantly ruminate about our individual and collective past and worry about a future that hasn't arrived yet. This causes deep suffering in the moment and shapes our future with well-worn anxiety habits.

When these moments of fear and uncertainty arise, whether related to being Jewish or not, many of our patterned Jewish responses do not serve us. In fact, they can be counterproductive to forming and strengthening compassionate, loving, and kind relationships with ourselves and with other people, many of whom might be our allies and beloveds. They can serve as unhelpful, habitual shields from being vulnerable, present, and open to what is happening in the present moment. These patterns create harm and suffering—first and foremost in our own lives and then ripple out into our communities and the wider world.

In this book, I ask some hard questions: What do we get by assuming the worst thing will happen, when that is not necessarily the case? What is the result of our internal and external catastrophizing, our ruminating, and worrying? What do we get by avoiding or distracting ourselves? What are we trying to prove by overworking and pushing ourselves to exhaustion? What happens when we project our fears, uncertainties, and anxieties on others by policing the boundaries of who is worthy of love, care, and belonging? These patterns are not helpful. Yet they are choices we make, repeatedly, without awareness of the harm we cause to ourselves and others. We have other choices that can offer us more joy, and less suffering.

In the very first chapter of *Pirkei Avot* (Ethics of Our Ancestors) 1:14, Rabbi Hillel says, "If I am not for myself, who will be for me? But if I am only for myself, who am I? And if not now, when?"[2] If we don't care for ourselves by attending to our anxiety and suffering with lovingkindness and compassion, who else can and will do that?

When we take care of ourselves, by examining our anxiety habits that cause us suffering, we can also care for our loved ones, friends, and our wider communities with those different habits: lovingkindness and compassion, instead of fear, anxiety, and judgment. This can create a different ripple effect in how we individually and collectively respond to the fear, uncertainty, and unpredictability of being Jewish in a difficult world.

Unlearning Jewish Anxiety is about noticing our inherited, deeply ingrained, sometimes unconscious, and culturally patterned responses that trigger fears about our safety and security, our "enough-ness," and our belonging. My hope is to help you notice these learned cultural habits and how these habits cause suffering in our bodies, our inner lives, relationships, and communities. *Unlearning Jewish Anxiety* offers a framework for understanding our learned habits, and where they come from, and why they might have served as adaptive responses in the past but cause us potentially unnecessary pain in the present.

I have included selections from the dozens of interviews I've conducted over the last several years in these pages. You will know when you come upon one of these because we have styled them in italics—so that these other Jewish voices stand out. In each instance, I note the speaker's pseudonym, or abbreviation for their name if they preferred to remain anonymous, as well as the decade of their age (i.e. "forties," "sixties," etc.) I also offer my own Jewish ways to turn the experience of our bodies, our lives and the world from places of constriction and tension into moments of more kindness, compassion, and ease. My hope is that we can unlearn our habits and open ourselves up to possibilities of joy, expansion, and spaciousness.

I wrote this book because I needed to change my own life, and I want to share my experiences, insights and tools from our rich Jewish spiritual inheritance with you. I hope that this book will provide some *aha!* moments of recognition about your own habits and patterns, not for you to judge with harsh criticism, but to soften with kindness, compassion, and better alternatives. My hope is you nod your head and feel seen. My greatest prayer is that you come to see that habits you might have learned from your family and community are not your fault—it's true that we live in a world filled with anti-Jewish oppression that makes us deeply anxious.

A famous aphorism attributed to Rabbi Nachman of Breslov opens this book. It says that "the whole world is a very narrow bridge, but the most important thing is to not be afraid." The *ikar*—the most important thing—of this book is to recognize that we each have choices in how to respond to the world, especially when we feel afraid or uncertain. We might not be able to solve the persistent challenge of anti-Jewish oppression in our lifetimes. But we come from a long ancestral tradition that values kindness and compassion, and healing what's broken in the world. We can learn how to develop new habits of kindness and compassion for ourselves, to heal ourselves. And by practicing new habits of kindness and compassion, we can change and heal the world.

kindness, compassion, and better alternatives. In part, you need to heal and reset [illegible] that you [illegible] from your daily [illegible] [illegible] world filled with [illegible].

A famous [illegible] [illegible] "It's not that [illegible] the world is a [illegible] [illegible] but [illegible] important [illegible] ahead." This [illegible] of this book is to [illegible] that we each have [illegible] the world [illegible] when we [illegible] uncertain. [illegible] challenge [illegible] life [illegible] [illegible] can change and heal the world.

Introduction

JEWISH ANXIETY IS REAL, AND YOU'RE NOT ALONE

I wish my anxiety wasn't so crippling, and crippling is right where I need to be working. I've closed a lot of doors because of my anxiety, and my world is pretty small. I wish I didn't have all of these anxieties so that my world could be bigger.

—Y., sixties

I would say that anxiety is deeply, innately, and genetically in my family, I've inherited it. I've been aware of my anxiety since I was very young—I could name it and identify it from the time I was seven, so I've been working on it. Compared to others in my family, I have amazing

What would your life feel like if you were less anxious? How would it feel to experience more joy, not because you've worked hard enough to earn it, but simply because you're alive? Jewish anxiety is a terrible, sneaky thief. It steals our joy. It shrinks our world and constricts our imagination of what's possible.

Maybe you're reading this because the title made you laugh with recognition. Maybe most days you feel generally anxious, restless, or uneasy, but you don't know why. Or maybe you know someone Jewish and anxious in your life and you're curious to understand more. Whatever the reason, I'm so glad you're here. I hope this book *awareness and control and have grown with it. It's all about fear of failure, not pursuing things because of anxiety, not working on oneself because of anxiety, the crippling experience of it.*

—Ali, forties

I feel like I have always had some baseline level of anxiety. So much of my parents' lives is dictated by fear and planning for adverse potential circumstances. I realized that it's been passed down to me. I think my anxiety keeps me from doing as many things as I would like to and participating in the world in a way that would be healthier.

—Shoshana, thirties

offers you some insight, practical tools, and relief.

I wrote this out of necessity, because I lived with disabling anxiety for most of my life, without awareness. A few years ago, I realized how much my anxiety came from how I grew up Jewishly, and how I respond to stress in identifiably Jewish ways. After teaching this material for several years and interviewing forty Jews across the United States, representing the Jewish denominational spectrum, and generations, I've learned that I'm not alone, and neither are you.[3] I write to show there are other ways to be Jewish in the world beyond anxiety. We can free ourselves with awareness, compassion, and practice.

So many Jews experience persistent, debilitating anxiety, and we laugh it off as inevitable, as just a fact of being Jewish. We learn early on how to act smaller than we are, to take up less space, keep quiet, be good, and please others. Some of this suffering is the legacy of our inherited, intergenerational trauma. Some of this suffering is an understandable response to deeply entrenched anti-Jewish contempt and violence in the world. When we don't feel safe, worthy of care and respect, and when we worry about whether we truly belong, life can feel deeply anxiety-provoking.

Learning to become anxious is not our fault. Anti-Jewish contempt is real, pernicious, and pervasive. It's difficult to be Jewish when people routinely express ambivalence and hostility toward our existence. And so *Unlearning Jewish Anxiety* focuses first on the

Jewish value of *tikkun atzmi*—healing ourselves, by taking responsibility for how we respond to that challenging reality and caring for ourselves with kindness and compassion. Then, when we care for ourselves, we become better resourced to address *tikkun olam*—the Jewish value of repairing our broken world.[4]

I reject the idea that anxiety is our birthright. Nor do I think we should tout Jewish anxiety as virtuously contributing to our collective and individual successes. Our anxiety robs us of making different choices to live in the present moment with more awareness, ease, pleasure, and calm. I know, from my own lived experience, that we can heal our anxiety habits to free up space in our lives for other things, like joy, creativity, and collective action.

Anxiety is also deeply unpleasant. When we feel anxious, we often want to *do something*, anything, to make those uncomfortable, difficult feelings go away. Anxiety causes deep suffering—in our minds, in our bodies, in our relationships with ourselves, and in our relationships with other people and the wider world. I believe it's *aleinu*—it's upon us, it's our responsibility to look at our habits that unwittingly amplify suffering.[5] It's our responsibility to nourish and care for ourselves, to honor our needs for safety, love, acceptance, and belonging. It's up to us to nurture our bodies and our spirit, especially in difficult times, such as the one we're currently living through. It's up to us to take responsibility for our own healing from the suffering we inherited, the anxiety we carry each day, and the anxious patterns we transmit to others in our families and Jewish communities. I believe that when we change our habits, we can suffer less and change our lives. When we change our lives, we create space to change the world.

MY BIG WHY

Anxiety runs deep in my Jewish family history, but I only realized this in my late forties. I didn't understand how my exposure to inherited, intergenerational trauma amplified my anxiety. I didn't understand how I unwittingly carried around vicarious Jewish trauma by constantly scanning the headlines for bad news about Jews. And finally, while I did encounter many moments of anti-Jewish contempt, I didn't connect the dots about how the accumulation of these experiences contributed to my own anxiety, stress, and internal shame about being othered.

We all live with kaleidoscopic identities—we're not just Jewish, we're complicated. We identify in so many other ways, and we live in a world that tries to compress, deny, or erase those complexities. Here's the kaleidoscope of who I am, which informs, and limits, how I experience and talk about Jewish anxiety in this book. I live as an Ashkenazi, upper-middle class, Gen X, queer, feminist, neurotypical, cis-gendered woman, with light skin, curves and curly textured hair. In the United States, I usually, although not always, pass as white. I live with multiple sclerosis, a largely invisible, yet impactful chronic illness. I am a survivor of sexual assault and have worked hard to overcome post-traumatic stress disorder engendered by that experience. As a rabbi, I deal with sexism inside and outside the Jewish community *all the time.* I recognize that you might walk through the world with different skin color, gender, generational or class identities, or abilities, or illnesses. Consider this book as an invitation for you to deepen the analysis and conversation here with your own lived experiences and perspectives.

I grew up in the upper middle-class suburbs of Chicago, in a community of immigrant, first- and second-generation Ashkenazi Jews. My working-class great-grandparents, and my maternal grandfather, immigrated from Poland and the Ukraine. These ancestors navigated pernicious anti-Jewish oppression and white supremacy, and they eagerly embraced assimilation. For example, my maternal grandfather left Poland at the age of three with his mother and brother. He grew up in Mexico City, came to the United States as a young adult. He became a naturalized citizen, tried to shed his Yiddish-inflected Spanish accent, and changed his name from Yossel Leibl Itzkowitz to George Louis to ameliorate the anti-Jewish harassment he experienced during his army service in the second World War. Growing up, the phrases I heard all the time, especially from my grandparents, were variations of "Don't make trouble, keep your head down, don't rock the boat." In other words, blend in with white folks, get a good education, make a good living, and don't draw too much attention to yourself, because it might spell trouble for the Jews. What I didn't realize was everyone in my family has suffered from Jewish anxiety: fear of anti-Jewish violence against us, fear that we weren't really accepted as American, fear that we didn't or might not really belong. I didn't know this consciously; it was simply the air I breathed.

I share this because all my ancestors made concerted efforts to shed their Jewish distinctiveness, become white, and accumulate wealth through education, work, and property. This becomes relevant in Chapter 3, where I examine the legacies of Jewish assimilation, internalized shame, and how this manifests as Jewish anxiety about acceptance, inclusion, and belonging.

Sadly, those patterns of fear, anxiety, and uncertainty influenced my first career as a university professor. I lived with a debilitating case of imposter syndrome. I worried that I wasn't smart enough and didn't belong in academia—when were people going to find that out? I suffered from panic attacks, learned to squelch my authentic writing voice, and struggled to finish my dissertation. I overworked *incessantly*. I went to the hospital a couple of times for chest pain, not realizing I was anxious. Once I even broke out into hives contemplating how I was going to grade seventy-five papers, finish a syllabus, and write a conference presentation in one weekend.

I kept up this manic pace for the next two decades. My anxiety manifested as perfectionism, the desire for control, fear of not being good enough, and keeping a relentless schedule of doing, doing, doing. I usually said yes to every opportunity that came my way because I worried "What if I say no?" and assumed the worst would happen if I set limits. I never gave myself permission to rest and simply be. I was exhausted all the time.

My anxiety came to a breaking point in late 2021. Along with so many of us, the pandemic took a toll on my physical and mental health. My back was tight all the time. I couldn't concentrate at work, and I wasn't sleeping well. I would obsessively check the COVID dashboard on the *New York Times*. During that terrible time, I discovered a fantastic book called *Unwinding Anxiety: New Science Shows How to Break the Cycles of Worry and Fear to Heal Your Mind*, written by Dr. Judson Brewer, a neuroscientist and mindfulness practitioner.[6] Over the next two years, Dr. Jud's work became a resource for my emotional and spiritual turn away from anxiety, and his work has influenced this book in countless ways.

In February 2022, I went for a walk, thinking about all the ways I've felt afraid, uncertain, and anxious. Then I had an epiphany: "OH MY GOD, IT'S NOT JUST ME! ALL MY FELLOW JEWS ARE SO ANXIOUS!" I realized everyone in my family, and many of my friends, colleagues, and congregants suffered from some clearly identifiable anxiety patterns. I started to wonder why so many Jews struggle with anxiety and how might relates to our culturally specific, habitual responses to stress, fear, and uncertainty. I knew intuitively, and from my own experience, that Judaism and Jewish spiritual practices could offer some resources to help us.

Through lots of spiritual and emotional effort to unlearn my own anxiety habits, I've come to believe that we Jews are worthy of safety, love, belonging and joy, *simply because we exist.* This feels like a radical claim in an era where so much ugly anti-Jewish rhetoric is visible in social media, and where claims of anti-Jewish contempt are weaponized for authoritarian purposes in our political discourse. Insisting that we are worthy of safety, love, belonging, and joy feels like a contradiction to everything I unconsciously learned growing up Jewish in the U.S.

I have learned how to identify my own deeply ingrained anxiety patterns, and how these habits are rooted in Jewish history and culture. I've observed how we communally perceive threats to our safety in ways that amplify our anxiety and suffering. I've noticed how many Jews automatically catastrophize and assume the worst will happen, because the worst already happened. I've also figured out how to loosen the grip of anxiety through what I call *kindfulness*: practicing present-moment awareness, kindness, compassion, and curiosity, through Jewish spiritual practices of pausing, breathing, and listening to our inner voice. My life is by no means entirely anxiety-free (whose is?), but I can say that through daily practice, *change is possible.* My hope is that by writing this book, you too can notice and unlearn your own anxiety habits too and live with more joy.

WHAT THIS BOOK IS AND IS NOT ABOUT

This book is about *tikkun atzmi*: healing ourselves so that we might suffer less. It's also about how our own unlearning might impact collective changes in our responses to anti-Jewish contempt, in service of *tikkun olam*—repairing our world. It's about becoming aware of, and turning away from, the habits we carry that reflect internalized shame and the cumulative trauma of anti-Jewish oppression. It's about becoming aware of and compassionate towards our own anxiety habits we've inherited and that we transmit generationally in our families and communities. It's about recognizing that our anxiety habits are understandable, but maladaptive strategies to cope with external oppression and stress. I believe we can assert our power and agency, individually and communally, to choose away from anxiety as a default response to anti-Jewish oppression. Ultimately, this book is about helping ourselves heal from habits that cause us suffering, to create space for more joy. When we transform our habits, we can heal and change our lives. When we change our lives and become freer from internalized oppression, we can engage in *tikkun olam*, healing and changing the world.

This book is not about eliminating the very real, frightening phenomenon of anti-Jewish contempt and oppression. Addressing anti-Jewish contempt in the wider world is indeed a worthy goal, but it's not my focus here. Honestly, I don't know whether it's possible to eliminate anti-Jewish contempt, given how it mutates and morphs over time. I do know, from talking with colleagues who work in this field, that it's exhausting and traumatizing to professionally deal with anti-Jewish oppression every day, all day long. My contribution here is to help *us* deal with the pernicious, internalized effects of that contempt, and how it shows up in our bodies, minds, thoughts, feelings, and habits.

You might have already noticed that I don't use the word antisemitism, but rather anti-Jewish oppression or anti-Jewish contempt. This is deliberate. The word antisemitism, coined by a nineteenth-century German Jew-hater named Wilhelm Marr, adopted a racial framework to justify hatred and systemic discrimination against Jews. In 1879, Marr founded the League of Antisemites, and his ideas later influenced Nazi thought and policies.[7]

I find this puzzling. We use a term, coined by someone who promulgated anti-Jewish contempt, to describe what *we* experience, using language (Semite) that no Jew uses to describe themselves. Personally, I refuse to give away my power to name what I know from lived experience, and from decades of learning and teaching about our complicated history and culture. I want us Jews to reclaim and change the language we use for what we see, feel and experience. This is why I use the words *anti-Jewish* contempt, disgust, and oppression throughout the book. Ultimately, this phenomenon rests on irrational anger, fear, revulsion, and conspiracy theories about and towards Jews that results in violence and oppression. Let's not use the language of someone who hated us. Let's call it what it is.

WHO THIS IS FOR

If you grew up Jewish, maybe you felt bored in religious school. Maybe now, if you have kids of your own, you feel confused, unclear, or ambivalent about your relationship to Judaism. Perhaps you grew up secular and identify as Jew-*ish* (said with a shrug), but the mere suggestion of doing anything "too Jewish" today makes you feel a little anxious, uncomfortable, or alienated. Maybe you lead a conversation about your Jewishness with "I'm spiritual, but not religious," or "I'm a bad Jewish because I (fill in the blank: eat bacon, don't go to synagogue, don't believe in God, etc.). Maybe you've got a nagging inner critic that always says that somehow, you're "not Jewish enough." Maybe you feel anxious about how much you feel like you don't know, and worry that everyone around you knows more, and judges you as not good enough to belong. Maybe you're yearning for some sort of spiritual connection with Jewish heritage, culture, or community, but every time you hear the word religious you conjure up a male Orthodox rabbi with a beard and feel anxious. Maybe when every autumn rolls around, you get a tight, anxious feeling about what to do about the High Holidays, that you're somehow obligated to attend long services in a language you don't understand, at a synagogue or temple you never attend the rest of the year. Maybe during those services you secretly check your phone in the bathroom when you've got *shpilkes* (ants in your pants). Does any of this sound familiar? This book is for you.

Perhaps you've got a different set of Jewish anxiety habits. Maybe you grew up with a strong Jewish connection and suffer from the distressing habits of perfectionism or the need to control everything so that it's done "right." Maybe the anxiety of all the planning and work it takes to observe Passover makes you feel exhausted and resentful, and by the end of the holiday you're so tired it doesn't feel much like a festival of freedom. Maybe you feel deeply anxious every time an anti-Jewish act of violence or vandalism or harassment is reported in the news and it makes you feel unsafe in the world. Maybe when you encounter different ways of doing and being Jewish, you hear a judgmental voice in your head that says, that's not the *right* way to do XYZ, or that's not *really* Jewish, when in fact, it's simply a different way of doing or being Jewish than how you grew up. If any of these patterns resonate with you, this book is for you.

This book is for you if you identify as Jewish and live in the United States or Canada as a minority (ethnic, cultural, religious) in a Christian-dominant society. This book is for you if you identify as Jewish and inhabit a body that experiences oppression or marginalization in ways that intersect with all the different ways of being Jewish and other kaleidoscopic identities in North America. If you are a Jewish person of color, some of the anxiety patterns around safety, worthiness, and acceptance might resonate in specific ways because of the intertwined, lived experiences of anti-Black racism and anti-Jewish oppression in this country. If you are a Jewish woman, if you are queer, or trans (and/or a person of color), if you are differently abled and/or live with chronic illnesses, these ideas might resonate in particular ways because of deeply entrenched sexism, homophobia, ableism, and anti-trans oppression. If you are Jewish and grew up poor or working class, the anxiety patterns about being/having enough, feeling acceptance and sense of belonging, and feeling safe might intertwine in particular ways with your lived experience.

WHAT IF I'M A CONVERT?

If you are a Jew by choice (and we all are, at this point in history), this book is for you too. You are uniquely situated to see the anxiety habits and patterns of your chosen community and culture(s) from the vantage point of not having grown up swimming in this anxious water. You might even notice different ways you've adopted Jewish anxiety habits to feel a sense of belonging and acceptance among anxious Jews. Not to worry—all these patterns are learned over time, which means they can be unlearned, through noticing with curiosity, holding ourselves with tenderness and compassion, and finding better alternatives to those habits that cause us suffering.

WHAT IF I'M A JEWISH ALLY OR MY PARTNER IS JEWISH AND I'M NOT?

If you're reading this far, and you've got Jewish loved ones in your life, bravo for picking up this book! This is for you too. Hopefully, you'll learn how to see your loved ones' habits and patterns through a broader lens of Jewish history and culture. You'll also learn how all our brains and bodies respond to stress, and how the stress of being othered as Jews creates distinctive patterns that connect to safety, worth, and belonging in an uncertain world. And finally, you'll learn lots of practical tools and concepts for how anyone, whether Jewish or from another spiritual tradition, can practice the qualities of awareness, kindness, compassion, and courage to respond differently when stressful situations arise.

Finally, *Unlearning Jewish Anxiety* is about learning how Jewish stress, trauma, and habits shape our lives as Jews. I offer a political analysis about how inherited Jewish trauma and internalized anti-Jewish oppression become lodged in our bodies and response patterns. I'll identify several common Jewish anxiety patterns, how they manifest in our bodies, our internal conversations with ourselves, and across our communal conversations about safety, worth, and belonging. And I will offer a framework, grounded in Jewish texts, values, and practices, that you can use to identify and unlearn your Jewish anxiety habits. You'll learn how to choose better alternatives that can provide a pause for your nervous system, ground you in the present moment, breathe, and simply *be.*

The Hebrew word and prayer *aleinu* means "it is upon us." It's a relevant frame how we might heal our Jewish anxiety. I think it's up to us, *aleinu,* to liberate ourselves from habitual suffering. We can choose away from getting stuck in habit loops that cause us distress. We can pause to discern better alternatives to our usual choices. We can redirect all that energy towards healing ourselves and changing the world in partnership with others. We can free up our individual and collective energy for more joy, creativity, liberation, expansiveness, activism, or whatever we're yearning for in our lives. I believe we can become more present for all the blessings that life offers us.

Chapter 1

THE NEUROSCIENCE OF ANXIETY AND HABITS

I think my anxiety is mostly suffering and not helpful to me. I can't think of one example of where I've felt anxious and it served a purpose for me, it's really a waste of time, because I'm going to take care of stuff anyway. It's like having a third elbow.

—Adam, late thirties

Anxiety sometimes feels all consuming. It's really hard to be present and in my body and just experience life. It feels like there's a wall around me that I can't feel joy, that I have to earn joy.

—Shelley, mid-forties

It's a beautiful Friday around noon, in late summer 2024. I'm driving home on the highway towards Denver after a short, early morning hike in the foothills of the Rocky Mountains. I look in my rearview mirror and see there's a guy driving a big black truck close to my bumper, honking his horn. Why is he driving so close and honking so insistently? I'm driving at the speed limit and there's plenty of room for him to pass me on the left. As traffic slows closer to the city, he pulls up to my left, and lowers his left window down, gesturing while honking. I get scared. I crack my window open (why???), and he yells out: "Hey, are you Jewish?" I freeze, feel afraid, and stammer slowly, "Why do

When things are going well, I worry whether things will last. I wonder when the other shoe is going to drop. I wish I could be completely in the moment, but I'm not, I'm worried about what might happen, that something might go wrong. I think it robs us of fully immersing ourselves in the joy of what's happening.

—Kaila, fifties

Anxiety is the number one source of all my pain. I'm very high anxiety and have been most of my life. I forget about it because it's a constant companion. It's always there. It's had an effect on me—it doesn't stop me from doing anything, but it robs me of my enjoyment of activities. Like socially or a work opportunity. It's a constant game of worst-case scenarios. When I've had a project not go well, I'll spin my wheels and not sleep about what ifs, and I jump to worst case scenarios. I just constantly ruminate and worry. The worst-case scenarios are rough. Beyond that, I think the second biggest thing is it's very hard to be present. I live so much in the future. I'll jump ahead too far and forget to live in the present moment.

—Eitan, forties

you ask? Are you Jewish?" I think to myself—does he have a gun? Is he a Jew-hater? Is he a Christian evangelical who is into Jews (it's a thing in Colorado)? Why would a stranger ask me this while driving on the highway?

Then I remember: I have a discreet Kamala Harris sticker on my bumper. It's the shape of a comma, with the Hebrew letters *lamed hey,* which spells "la." The guy clearly understood the sticker, and he says, "Of course I'm Jewish, I'm Israeli!" and he shows me the black kippah on his head. He says, "Shabbat shalom!" with a smile and a wave, and drives off. I manage to mumble a weak "Shabbat shalom" back to him with relief. Then I close the window, exhale, and realize my heart is pounding in my chest. This is what Jewish anxiety looks like.

ANXIETY 101: FEAR AND UNCERTAINTY

When I teach about unlearning Jewish anxiety, I ask students how anxiety shows up in their bodies. They do not hesitate, offering detailed and vivid descriptions of their lived experiences. Usually, they refer to some part of their body feeling tight, like their jaw, chest, neck, shoulders, or back.

For me, anxiety is tightness. It's that wave of everything in my body tingling in towards the center line – my throat, heart, and chest. It comes on feeling like tingling and numbness and the tightness remains and is holding on. I've gotten dizzy, and once I was convinced that I had a brain tumor. When it subsides, then it's digestive.

—Ruti, forties

The people I interviewed described tingling and numbness in their hands and feet, dizziness, or gastrointestinal distress. Sometimes my students talk explicitly about being Jewish as a source of their anxiety, and at other times, they talk more generally. This is not surprising—when we experience oppression in the world, it's hard to untangle why we feel so stressed out and tight in our bodies. Fear, uncertainty, stress, and oppression are complicated and intertwined.

Anxiety arises as a physical response when we navigate situations where we feel afraid, uncertain, unsafe, excluded, threatened or othered as different and unequal. Anxiety is an evolutionary, embodied reaction to perceived threats—such as the use of power by others, in a way that potentially and adversely impacts our safety and well-being in the world. When we feel fear, an ancient part of our brains—our amygdala—registers this as a perceived threat to our survival.

Fear is one of the oldest and strongest emotions we experience. Fear helps us learn what is safe, what is dangerous, and how to avoid or escape situations where we might be in danger. Fear creates powerful neural grooves in our brain to increase the chances for survival. Here's one example of how I learned from a fearful experience.

I love to go hiking by myself in the mountains, and I also happen to love singing Broadway musical soundtracks when I'm in nature. Several years ago, I had a chance encounter with a very large moose on the trail in Rocky Mountain National Park while singing the lyrics to *Hamilton*. It was awesome, in the sense that I had never seen a moose so nearby. It was also utterly terrifying. When the moose and I made eye contact, I felt panicky. My heart was racing, and my breathing got ragged. I froze, not knowing what to do. Then I slowly backed away from the stream where the moose was lounging on the other side. When I was several hundred yards away, I ran as fast as I could in the opposite direction. When I stopped running, my body was pouring sweat, but I felt chilled. It took about an hour for my nervous system to calm down. The evolutionary takeaway for my scared amygdala: I would never, ever wear ear buds again when hiking alone. Lesson learned, I survived, and this prompted a new habit.

Our brains help us stay safe when we experience a situation that involves fear and uncertainty. This becomes relevant when thinking about Jewish anxiety, because we often feel scared and triggered by being *othered,* like being asked whether we're Jewish by a stranger on the highway (who ironically, was Jewish). Our amygdala kicks in with adrenaline and cortisol—stress hormones that activate our nervous system to help us survive a perceived threat. Our vision of what's happening narrows. Our bodies get tight. Then we respond to stimuli in survival mode, not from logic. From an evolutionary standpoint, the newer part of our brain, called the Posterior Cingular Cortex (or PCC for short) goes offline. Our PCC is responsible for logic, reasoning, spatial navigation, and decision-making. Neuroscientists hypothesize that the PCC is involved in self-referential activities, like retrieving our memories, as well as engaging in future-oriented planning. It's also what we call, in popular psychology, the part of our brain that makes us feel self-conscious and highly aware of our individual self, known as the "I," or the ego.

When we're responding to stimuli in our environment from our amygdala, we move into high arousal and hyper-vigilance. Our hearts race, our muscles contract, we get sweaty, our breathing becomes rapid, we might feel hot or cold, we might feel shaky or panicky. We might feel tightness in our chest, a stiffening of our spine, clenching in our jaws and butts, or racing thoughts. This response makes us want to *DO SOMETHING* to deal with the sense of threat.

THE FOUR "F" RESPONSES TO FEAR AND UNCERTAINTY

I grew up in Salt Lake City, and there were very few Jews at the time. I remember going to class right after the Six Day War ended in Israel. A couple of kids were staring at me, and one of the kids said something about how we really kicked butt against those people, they said, "Y'all were so tough!" I had a surge of pride in me that for once, we (as Jews) were ok. When I got in fights, I wanted to fight back with everything I had. I remember that feeling of walking in and feeling proud that whole week—as if I had anything to do with it. I didn't have a lot of pride about being Jewish as a child.

—Roger, seventies

The most common way to understand that impulse to *do something* is the Four F's: fight, flight, freeze, and fawn (people please, to avoid being harmed). Pete Walker, a therapist and author of *Complex PTSD: From Surviving to Thriving,* offers a concise description of the fight, flight, freeze, and fawn responses of our nervous systems. He writes:

> A fight response is triggered when a person suddenly responds aggressively to something threatening. A flight response is when a person responds to a perceived threat by fleeing, or symbolically, by launching into hyperactivity. A freeze response is triggered when a person, realizing resistance is futile, gives up, numbs out into dissociation, and/or collapses, as if accepting the inevitability of being hurt. A fawn response is triggered when a person responds to threats by trying to be pleasing or helpful to appease or forestall an attacker.[8]

How we respond to the perception of threat is also influenced by *politics*: by the unequal and unfair distribution of power in the world, by the different identities we hold, and the different experiences of oppression we carry. When we fear or perceive that we are being othered or threatened as Jews (or as part of another group), this oppression-stress activates our amygdala. We jump into hyper-arousal, hypo-arousal, hyper-vigilance, and high reactivity. It's understandable that we want to keep ourselves safe from the stressful feeling of threat. My most common stress responses to oppression are flight, freeze, and fawn. I usually want to run away, or I simply don't know what to do or say. Sometimes I have disassociated by pretending something didn't just happen, or I have used humor and flattery to deflect my discomfort or fear, or I try to leave the situation if possible. A fight response does not come naturally to me, and I've always wondered if that's because I've been socialized as a woman to be a "good girl," i.e., polite and nice.

Here are some Jewish examples: when Donald Trump was first elected in 2016, I remember feeling so threatened, afraid, and agitated that I immediately googled how to move to Canada or New Zealand (a flight response). I had insomnia for months, pacing with worry about all the what if scenarios in the middle of the night, doomscrolling the news on my phone. These were understandable responses to my fear, sense of threat, and uncertainty about the future. I didn't know at the time, but my habits were only ramping up my anxiety, not alleviating it. Do any of these responses sound familiar? If yes, you are not alone.

I invite you to take a moment now to reflect on your own experience of the four "Fs." Think of a situation (maybe a 4 on a scale of 1-10) where you felt uneasy, uncertain, or a little afraid. How did that fear or uncertainty show up in your body? What did you notice about your breathing, if you remember anything? What kinds of thoughts or feelings came up for you in that situation? What kind of response did you deploy to keep yourself safe? If you can pull up a memory of what was happening in your body (for example, discomfort, a racing heart, shaking, cold sweat, numbness or tingling, tightness in your body), that's a somatic, embodied memory of your amygdala responding to a perceived threat, helping you to stay safe. When we feel tightness, contraction, stiffening, racing heartbeats and sweating these are important *embodied* clues to signal that our PCC is offline and we're in survival mode from our amygdala.

If you take time out right now to reflect, please be gentle with yourself—bringing up memories of feeling anxious, afraid, or stressed out can re-activate our nervous systems. Take a few moments to breathe. Remember that right now, you're safe. These responses, memories, and experiences were your brain and body trying to keep you safe. You're ok right now. You might want to take a break from reading the next section for another time when your nervous system has had a chance to settle down.

HABITS: AN IMPORTANT PIECE IN THE ANXIETY PUZZLE

How we respond to fear and uncertainty from our amygdala are the first two pieces in understanding anxiety. The third piece is all about our habits: repetitive behaviors we do for efficiency's sake, to help us create structure and order in our lives without having to re-learn every little task. To mitigate the exhausting possibility of brain fatigue associated with constant relearning, we ingenious humans create habits. Our habits can be great tools to meet our needs for structure, predictability, routine, consistency and stability. Habits help us feel more in control of our lives. Sometimes we're consciously involved in a habit, but more often than not, we're not even aware of how we're responding to something out of habit. That's the beauty of habits: sometimes we hardly notice them, because they're so repetitive, efficient, and unconscious.

Think of your own habits when you first wake up in the morning.

Maybe you stretch while in bed. Maybe you get up and immediately turn on your coffee before doing anything else. Maybe the first thing you do when you come to consciousness is to think worry thoughts about your to-do list or check your phone.

My morning habits are influenced by Jewish spirituality and the work of Dr. B.J. Fogg, author of *Tiny Habits: The Small Changes that Change Everything.*[9] Fogg suggests that we break down a habit into the tiniest pieces to make changes more realistic and feasible. I wanted to begin my day with gratitude and kindness. To start a new habit, I decided that before I put my feet on the floor, I would say a Jewish gratitude prayer, called *Modah Ani* for having another day to live. Then I would myself a hug and say, "I love you and today is going to be a great day." I know that sounds cheesy, but I have found these tiny changes highly impactful, because they are so easy, and they give me a boost of positive energy first thing in the morning. After a few weeks of this habit, I decided to build on it. I would head to the kitchen, turn on the coffee, and stretch in mindful meditation while the coffee brews. Again, it was only a tiny change—ten minutes of stretching to bring awareness to my body and breathe deeply. This routine is called habit stacking—stringing small habits together that result in positive outcomes. The result of my habit stacking: most mornings, I feel grateful, connected to my experience of the Divine and looser in my body. What are your early morning habits, and how do they make you feel in your body and your mind? Take a moment to write down a habit you do every day. What do you notice? What is the result of your habit?

Other examples of habits: how we brush and floss our teeth; how, where, and when we shop for groceries; what, when, why, and how much food we put into our mouths; what routes we take to get to work or school, what we do in our free time, and when, why, and how much we reach for our phones. So are the familiar and repetitive ways we react without thinking, to our parents, partners, children, co-workers, and friends. We also have many learned habits, some of which are unconscious, in response to fear, uncertainty, stress, or emotional triggers in life.

Judaism as a spiritual practice also creates lots of opportunities for habits, specifically ritual habits that revolve around the daily, weekly, monthly and yearly Jewish calendar. So much of what Jews repetitively do (or avoid doing) is through exercising habits that strengthen those spiritual and ritual muscle memories. For example, some of us begin each day with Jewish prayer. Some of Jews habitually think prayer is a crock because it requires belief in God as a king in the sky (foreshadowing hint: it doesn't, and we'll explore this later in Chapter 5). Some Jews observe Jewish holidays in familiar ways each year, and some Jews don't. Some of us light candles on Shabbat, say blessings, go to synagogue, and have a lovely meal as a spiritual habit. Some of us throw breadcrumbs into a body of water on Rosh Hashanah to symbolically release our mistakes and errors that caused harm over the past year. Some of us have adopted the habits of wearing white, and/or fasting on Yom Kippur to enhance our spiritual experience of practicing forgiveness and compassion for ourselves and others. If you're starting to feel stressed out because you don't do any of these habits and you're wondering whether you're Jewish enough—please take a deep breath. Feeling "not enough" or unworthy as a Jew is also a habit, and we'll explore how and why that's the case. We'll learn why some Jews resolutely reject doing anything Jewish as a habit because of their ancestors' assimilation strategies, their own past harmful experiences of exclusion, or being shamed by other Jews.

One of the most important things to understand about habits is the *outcome* of the routine: in behavioral science literature, it's known variously as a reward or a result (positive or negative). I use the word result rather than reward or outcome, because when we engage in harmful or negative habits, it's hard to think of that as a reward.

When the result of a habit feels good, our brain releases dopamine, a chemical that helps us learn how to pair memory of places, experiences, and feelings with those behaviors. For example, if you post a vacation photo to your social media and receive a gazillion likes, it produces a dopamine hit in your brain, to associate posting vacation photos with a positive result (I feel seen! People like me! I'm worthy!). You might continue to post vacation photos every time you travel, because of this positive association and reward.

This is why social media can feel so addictive; we get hooked to occasional and pleasurable hits of dopamine, even if the overall result of our consumption sometimes results in feeling lonely, jealous, or inadequate. Seeing other people's curated feeds often makes us feel worse because we engage in comparison thinking. We scroll for a while, start to feel awful, and finally put the phone down. Does this sound familiar?

I used to scroll unconsciously for years. After learning about anxiety habits through the work of Dr. Jud Brewer, I wondered what it would feel like to experience JOMO (the joy of missing out) instead of habitual FOMO. I wanted to feel more present in my life and spend less time on my phone. Now, instead of reaching for my phone when I feel bored, I notice the feeling until it passes. I observe what's happening in my body. I breathe for about ninety seconds to watch the sensations, thoughts, and feelings shift. In cognitive behavioral therapy literature, this practice is called urge surfing—you notice when the urge arises, focus on the sensations and feelings, and ride the waves of those feelings until they subside. Usually, the urge to check and scroll diminishes within sixty to ninety seconds.

The rewards of practicing urge surfing with my phone were profoundly beneficial. I felt calmer. I engaged in less self-flagellating comparison thinking. I had more time to practice meditation and movement, which also helped me feel calmer and clearer. In fact, the rewards were so awesome, I decided to limit my total daily phone usage to under two hours. Sometimes I'm successful, and sometimes not. But the result of this new habit is worth it. I feel freer. I'm more present. The good news is that you can apply these insights from neuroscience and behavioral science, whether you're working on a general or particularly Jewish anxiety habit. Let's now turn to the seven elements that create a habit.

Chapter 2

THE SEVEN ELEMENTS OF A HABIT

Charles Duhigg, in his 2014 book, *The Power of Habit: Why We Do What We Do in Life and Business,* popularized the science of habits to a wide audience.[10] He distilled habits down to three basic elements: a cue, a routine or behavior, and a result. This is a great start, and I think there's more to it that involves the body. Every day, we move through so many lightning quick, often unconscious cues that trigger our habits. We also experience a range of embodied sensations, a subterranean ocean of fleeting feelings, a seemingly endless stream of thoughts, and more importantly, a range of basic human needs that drive our behavioral habits. This chapter explores those elements of a habit loop that previous studies miss. To understand how habits work, I invite you to imagine the face of a clock, with ten-minute increments. For each of the following elements, we'll move to the next increment.

FIRST, THE CUE

This is the beginning of a habit: an event, a situation, or an interaction in your environment. This "cue" can be completely ordinary: your alarm goes off at 6:30am and you habitually reach for your phone (behavior). Your stomach growls, you look up from your laptop and realize you haven't eaten in three hours. It's 3pm and you need to pick up the kids from school.

A cue can be benign or neutral, something pleasant, or something unpleasant. Every day, we experience many internal and external cues that prompt our habits. To reiterate, the benefit of habits is that they can often help us get through the day efficiently without having to relearn or rethink how to respond in each moment of our lives. If we had to relearn how to brush our teeth, wash our hands, find our way to school, work or the grocery store, we would quickly get exhausted.

For this exercise, think of a cue that sets off a benign, neutral, or pleasant habit. On the clock in your imagination—or literally in front of you on the wall or dresser or, even better, on a piece of paper in front of you now—write the short description of that cue down at 12 o'clock at the top of the circle. Sometimes it's easier to begin understanding our habits with something easy and pleasant rather than going for the jugular of our most difficult habits with which we struggle. Leave it there, looking at it and considering it.

Now we'll move from the cue you've identified to the next ten-minute mark: sensations, thoughts, feelings, and needs. These sensations, thoughts, feelings, and needs might all be happening at once, without us even knowing it. But it's helpful to tease each one out, to better understand what's happening when you're inside a habit loop.

NOTICE SENSATIONS

This often begins with a sensation in the body, such as noticing when you're feeling tight, stressed, or stiff-necked. In the Torah, when Moses is frustrated, he describes the Israelites as a "stiff-necked people." I would agree. Many of us are not just stiff-necked: we also suffer from stiff lower backs, jaws, hips, joints, and muscles, not because our ancestors built a Golden Calf in the desert, but because we're anxious, and we experience this stiffness and anxiety unconsciously through sensations.

Sensations in our bodies are not just cues; they're the essential building blocks to create more awareness of what's happening in the present moment. The first step in building our awareness is to begin with our bodies and what embodied sensations tell us.[11] But many of us are not taught or encouraged to live in our bodies, and we simply live in our heads with an endless stream of feelings and thoughts that begin with sensations. We also experience sensations that arise in our bodies without our conscious awareness, without our mind labeling them as sensations, or as clues to how our habits make a powerful impact on our bodies. Connecting deeply with what's happening in our bodies is a powerful first step in unlearning. Here's one example.

In my previous career as a Jewish Studies professor, I commuted an hour each way from Denver to Boulder on a highway with lots of construction. On Wednesdays, I taught three challenging, large classes in a row. I developed a stacked habit on Tuesday nights: I would make my lunch and lay out my gym and work clothes to feel more organized in the morning. These behavior habits helped me feel grounded (a positive result). However, as I made my lunch and set out my clothes, I would have lots of anxious, worried thoughts and feelings about the following day that generated embodied sensations, of which I was completely unaware.

My Tuesday evening cue (make lunch for tomorrow, think about and prep lectures in my head) created a sensation of tightness in my left scapula, which grew progressively tighter and more painful over the course of the next twenty-four hours. Every Wednesday evening, after an exhausting twelve-hour day, I could barely move my neck and left shoulder. I don't blame myself for not noticing that my Tuesday night kicked off my worry habit that contributed to my stiff neck and frozen scapula. I didn't know about the neuroscience of habits yet, and I wasn't living much in my body, I lived in my head.

My point is that embodied sensations are pivotal clues to understanding any stress we might be experiencing in our bodies, whether our nervous system has unconsciously identified a source of stress or perceived threat. They're also a glimpse into our habits.

Let's return to your clock and the cue you've identified that prompts a habit. What is that habit, for you? When the cue begins, what do you notice in your body? Mark it on your clock at ten minutes past 12 o'clock. Do you feel relaxed when the cue prompts the habit? Are there any sensations that arise in response to the cue? Do you feel expansion or contraction, tightness or openness anywhere in your body when the cue begins? Take a few moments to write down your observations now.

NEXT, THE FEELINGS

Let's move to the twenty-minute mark on your habit clock: feelings. Some of us grow up in families where the expression of feelings (particularly vulnerable ones) was encouraged. I think many more of us grow up in families where the accepted vocabulary range of feelings might have been quite constrained.

Our ability to connect sensations to feelings depends on not just our familial culture, but also different identities. We learn to identify, express, or squelch our feelings based on those identities, the people around us, where we grew up, and what feelings are valued or considered dangerous. If you grew up Jewish, you were likely socialized into tacit norms about gender, sexual orientation, the expression of feelings, and Jewish culture.[12] In the community where I grew up, heterosexuality was compulsory, and girls were discouraged from expressing anger or sadness. So I learned to squelch my complicated feelings and retreat to my journal to write them out. I also learned to avoid and deflect my anger and sadness through fawning strategies, such as humor.

Psychologists identify six basic feelings: sadness, anger, surprise, disgust, fear, and happiness.[13] From these elemental feelings, more complex emotions arise, like restlessness or anxiety, humiliation or disappointment, hurt or vulnerability, trust and acceptance, for example. Growing your awareness of feelings is one of the most important steps you can take in an unlearning journey, because our feelings directly connect to our thoughts, needs, and behaviors when we're in an anxiety habit loop. Often, the behaviors we choose to address our unease, restlessness, discomfort, or distress, sometimes amplify those feelings, rather than diminish them.

Take a moment now to consider the habit you've identified, the cue, and the sensations in your body when it starts. What are some feelings that typically arise from that cue and those bodily sensations? Are they pleasant or unpleasant? Do those feelings generate a sense of tightness or constriction, or do they move towards openness and expansion? Here, you might want to enlist an online feelings wheel to get clear about the basic feeling and then fan out to notice the more complicated feelings that emerge from your habit cue and sensations. Then we're on to the connection between embodied sensations, feelings, and thoughts.

THOUGHTS: PAST, PRESENT, AND FUTURE

We're now at the thirty-minute mark of our habit clock: we're calling this 12:30. Our thoughts, whether conscious or unconscious, often drive our behaviors, actions, and decisions throughout our days. The truth is some of us are only dimly aware of the constant stream of our thoughts, many of which are negative, self-critical, ruminative about the past, or worries about the future. Sometimes our thoughts are easier to identify because we hear them in our heads. Here you might want to pause and to stop and consider those voices in your head, because they're often just *habitual thoughts,* and not necessarily reflective of reality.

Have you ever noticed that we're always talking to ourselves?

If you've ever sat for five minutes in meditation, or gone for a walk by yourself, you might have an awareness of your inner voice that's talking, talking, talking. Meditators of all levels of experience often notice when our attention has just wandered off into thoughts about lunch, about how uncomfortable our posture might feel, the dreams we had last night, the to-do list we're not getting to, or how bored we are. There's nothing wrong with talking to ourselves, it's what our minds do. Noticing with awareness that our thoughts have wandered is in fact the whole purpose of meditation.

What's also important in noticing our thoughts is that we're so often thinking about things that are not happening right now. Instead, we get caught up in thinking about the past. We ruminate on something that has happened that bothers us, or we review what we might have said or done differently. We chew on past hurts, or we remember that great vacation we just took and what a drag it is to navigate re-entry into ordinary life. We also habitually think unkind thoughts about who we are, which are usually untrue. Psychologists call it "the inner critic," and many of my students report living with a very loud, rude, and disparaging inner critic in their heads. What does your inner critic say to you? What does it feel like to experience those unkind, and probably untrue thoughts? For me, it wasn't fun, and it amplified my experience of anxiety.

We also spend vast amounts of time thinking about the future. We worry, we plan, and we fret about what *might* happen, but hasn't yet, because the future is never fully here. I have spent so many years of my life in an agitated state of negative thoughts about the past: fulminating, ruminating, regretting, and speechifying about things I could not and can't change, because they're in the past. I've also spent years of my life trying to stave off, prevent, or plan my way out of things that hadn't happened yet or were beyond my control. I recognize now, without blaming or shaming, that these habits of rumination and worry were something I learned from my family of origin and Jewish culture. These anxiety habits parachuted me out of whatever was happening in the present moment, and into the past that was gone, or the future that had not arrived yet.

Thinking about the past and the future often prompts lots of feelings that we're usually not aware of when we're in the throes of a habit, whether that habit is positive, neutral, or negative. It's a bit of chicken and egg: we might think about something a friend or family member said that hurt our feelings, and then we feel the hurt all over again and have more thoughts about why they were wrong, or how we feel misunderstood or not seen. When we have thoughts about the future (like my Tuesday night worry ritual), we might start to feel stressed out about things that haven't yet happened, or things beyond our control.

Again, the point here in disentangling these strands of sensations, feelings, and thoughts is not to berate or judge ourselves. It's to prompt more awareness of what happens when we're inside a habit. Take a moment now to return to your circle and you're at the thirty-minute mark of your clock. Try to identify some thoughts that come up when you're in the habit you want to learn from.

NEEDS: THE UNSPOKEN GIFT

We're now at the forty-minute mark on your habit clock, which is all about discerning what we need when we're in an anxiety habit. I've learned about needs from the work of Marshall Rosenberg, a Jewish psychologist and founder of the Center for Non-Violent Communication. Rosenberg grew up in the 1940s in Detroit, and experienced visceral anti-Jewish bullying and violence as a child. This shaped his understanding of himself as a Jew and deeply influenced his work. Rosenberg often talked about how our feelings can help us identify what we need from moment to moment, and how we can cultivate empathy and compassion for ourselves and others to resolve conflicts.[14]

Rosenberg's premise was that all human beings share basic

needs required to sustain and enrich our lives. These needs include sustenance, safety, love, understanding, empathy, creativity, worth (value, recognition, affirmation, and respect), a sense of belonging, autonomy (choice and control over our lives) and meaning. We also need beauty and joy, wholeness and harmony, trust and mutuality, fulfillment and well-being. There are several online resources about Rosenberg's constellation of needs you can explore to understand your own.

In Rosenberg's model of non-violent communication, when we're experiencing strong feelings, that's a sign to understand our met or unmet needs. We can learn how to identify our needs and choose different behaviors to meet them when we're looking to change our habits. When we identify what we need, we can discern the range of choices available to us in each moment. We can meet our own needs or ask others for help.

Good things happen when our basic needs are met. We feel spacious and expansive in our lives and our bodies. We feel more loving, peaceful, relaxed, energetic, joyful, warm, and content. When we have unmet needs, our experience of life feels quite different. We might feel scared, ashamed, heartbroken, helpless, agitated, impatient, or angry. In other words, when we're suffering, when we feel uncomfortable, upset, or anxious, our sensations, feelings, and thoughts are important signs of unmet needs.

For example, if you wake up exhausted from a poor night's sleep, you might need more rest. You might ask your partner to drop the kids off at school, re-arrange your day to catch a quick nap, or if that's not possible, you might order a latte with an extra shot to stay alert. If you get into a fight with a family member and feel upset, angry, or frustrated, it might point to an unmet need for feeling heard and understood. You might also have a need for *shalom bayit* - peace and harmony in your home and important relationships.

Why are needs so relevant to understanding our habits? The answer is simple: all habits fulfill a need, whether we know it or not.

If we didn't have a need to fulfill, we probably wouldn't engage in a behavior habit to satisfy the need. However, sometimes we don't know what we need. Or we ignore our own needs (women learn this early on in life), or we create habits that don't necessarily result in getting our needs met. It takes effort to understand how our habits fulfill a need.

To return to my Tuesday night university professor prep habit, the thought of having to sprint through a twelve-hour day felt so stressful. I needed to feel calm, grounded and prepared. I didn't love my work situation and had lots of feelings and negative thoughts about it. But I didn't realize these sensations, feelings, and thoughts were connected to unmet needs. All I knew at the time was that I didn't want to feel rushed to complete chores and then run late and rush up to Boulder with additional stress about fighting traffic or getting to class on time. I set up that Tuesday night habit out of a need for control in a situation that felt a bit out of control. I needed to feel confident that I could fulfill my teaching responsibilities. I needed a shorter, less stressful commute. But it took years to discern that my Tuesday night worry habits were not just about the commute, long days, and big classes. My job was not fulfilling some important needs, and after five years of discernment, I left the hamster wheel of academia and pivoted to the rabbinate. I needed to feel happier, calmer, more connected to purpose, and more fulfilled in my life's work.

When we slow down and pay attention to what might be driving our habits, we can get in touch with what we *really* need. This is especially the case when our nervous systems get triggered and go into fight, flight, freeze, or fawn mode because of stressors. How does this connect to internalized anti-Jewish oppression? The truth is, getting our needs met also connects to how much power we do or don't have in each situation, family system, school, workplace, organization, political system, and society. Getting our needs met is political.

Many of us might have grown up in families where we were not taught to identify, express, and advocate for our needs, or we were taught that our needs didn't matter. In my own life experience, if you navigate the world with any number of stigmatized or marginalized identities, you learn *not* to advocate for getting your needs met. You learn, through how people use or abuse power, that you might be rejected, shamed, harmed, excluded, rejected, or abandoned. We'll explore this phenomenon of unmet needs, power, and oppression much more in the next two chapters about how Jews internalize anti-Jewish oppression and learn to suppress our needs for safety, affirmation, and belonging.

For now, while you're examining your own habit, take a moment to go online and look up a needs wheel. Now that you've gotten clearer about the sensations, feelings, and thoughts when you're in your habit loop, can you identify what some of your needs might be? How are those needs connected to your inherent humanity, like the need for safety, affirmation of your worth, or a sense of belonging? We'll explore these needs, and how they show up in Jewish anxiety habits, much more in the next chapter.

BEHAVIORS: RESPONSE CHOICES

The next stop on the habit clock is our behavior. How many times throughout your day do you launch into a behavior or action without thinking much about other possible choices? Let's use familiar shared experience: waking up from the alarm on a weekday and feeling tired or stressed out about work or school. The alarm clock is the cue—it's 12 o'clock and time to wake up. The sensation you might feel in your body, before you even have a thought or feeling, is exhaustion (hello Friday mornings after a busy week!). You might feel resentful about having to wake up early. You might simply feel like you're still at the bottom of the ocean of sleep. You might think to yourself, *Ugh, I just want to turn over for another hour*. What might you need? More rest! Less stress!

You're at a choice point about behavior: you can press snooze or get up. You could also call in sick and just rest for the morning, depending on the circumstances. Perhaps you get up, because you need to meet a deadline, run a meeting, or take a test. Perhaps you get up and out of bed, despite your fatigue, because you want to stretch or exercise, or you need to walk the dog, or wake up the kids and take them to school. Perhaps you have more flexibility in your schedule, and you decide to turn off the alarm for one snooze. The point here is that we usually have a few choices available to us at each moment. But because our behavior habits become so automatic, we forget about the potential to make other choices based on our sensations, thoughts, feelings, and needs. Take a moment now to identify and write some of the behavior(s) you normally choose in the habit you're examining. What do you notice about how you typically respond to the cue, sensations, thoughts, feelings, and needs? What other behavior choices might you make in that moment? What are some possibilities you haven't thought of yet?

DISTRACTION AND AVOIDANCE: DETOURS TO SUFFERING

Let's pause for a moment in the habit loop to talk about the behavioral detours we take that engender more suffering. I love to read Buddhist and secular mindfulness texts about suffering, impermanence, and meditation, and incorporate this wisdom into my own Jewish practice. Some of my most important teachers have been Buddhist monks, in addition to many Jewish teachers of mindfulness. All these teachers focus on one of the most important Buddhist insights, what is called the first of Four Noble Truths: life is often uncomfortable, difficult, and filled with suffering. Judaism understands this too, albeit in different ways.

We all suffer, no matter whether or what we practice spiritually. Our bodies are vulnerable to injury and illness. We experience the painful loss of a loved one and move through what feel like endless waves of grief. We go through break-ups, divorce, and job losses. In this era of climate crisis, some of us lose our homes or livelihoods (or both) to catastrophic disasters such as fires, floods, tornados and hurricanes. We all eventually die. These are just a few of the obvious ways we navigate human suffering engendered by vulnerability, change, and the precarious uncertainty of life. This is why many spiritual habits and practices, whether Jewish or Buddhist, or another tradition, can help us respond to life's uncertainties with compassion and equanimity.

However, we often unconsciously choose to engage in distraction and avoidance behaviors that paradoxically *increase* our suffering. When we experience something unpleasant, uncertain, stressful, or frightening, our nervous systems respond with fight, flight, freeze, or fawn, ostensibly to help us survive. Distraction and avoidance behaviors are usually flight and freeze responses to temporarily relieve distress or discomfort through busyness or numbing out. Sadly, these flight and avoidance choices don't make our problems, our distress, discomfort, or our suffering, go away. Drinking alcohol, eating a gallon of ice cream, scrolling for hours, overworking, or binge-watching an entire series on Netflix might help us feel less distressed momentarily, but the difficult feelings (boredom, loneliness, pain) remain after we've put the drink or the phone down, or turned off the TV.

For example, I often read the *New York Times* after I've practiced gratitude, self-compassion, stretched and made coffee. When I read about national politics and violence unfolding in the Middle East, my stomach gets knotted, and I have the overwhelming urge to turn away and distract myself by checking social media. That's understandable. Reading about our country's political direction, and people suffering in a place I love and care about prompts my own suffering and anxiety. It makes me feel powerless and helpless. These are unpleasant feelings. Turning away to avoid the news and distract myself by scrolling through people's vacation and puppy photos does not make the suffering go away. And the avoidance and distraction of scrolling doesn't make me feel any better over the long term either. I simply avoid the discomfort and sorrow for a few minutes, but then I notice the grief, sadness, and anger returning. This has led me to identify a spin cycle habit of suffering that I'm still working on. Sometimes, I simply pause to breathe through the pain and grief, sending compassion towards myself and out into the world. Some days, I make monetary gifts of *tzedakah* (right action) or sign petitions to causes and organizations I care about. Other days, I pause to discern what I really need in that moment and make a choice to scan the headlines later in the day to give my nervous system a rest.

Sometimes, our habitual behavior choices simply reinforce the resulting stress we feel in our bodies, without meeting what we really need. Dr. Kristin Neff and Dr. Shauna Shapiro, researchers in the field of self-compassion argue that "what we practice gets stronger."[15] Every time we choose to engage in a behavior, it can become so efficient, so habitual, so automatic, we don't even notice we're doing it, *even when the results of that behavior are negative or harmful for us.*

Does any of this resonate with you? I imagine there are probably some distraction or avoidance habits you can easily identify that provide a momentary relief but don't address the underlying feelings of discomfort or distress. Take a moment now to identify one negative behavior habit of distraction or avoidance you might want to work on to map out your habit. When you've identified the behavior piece, ask yourself the question: what happens when you reach for that behavior? Taking the time to discern that answer brings us to the final element of a habit: the *results* of our behaviors.

RESULTS: OUTCOMES OF HABITS THAT SHAPE OUR LIVES

Now we're back at the top of the clock of our habit: the *results* of our thoughts, feelings, needs, and behaviors. Let's return to our example of waking up tired in the morning. What is the result of turning off the alarm and putting your feet on the floor? It might be a positive or negative result, depending on the circumstances. You might get the kids out the door and get yourself to work on time but be grumpy with your family and continue to feel exhausted and stressed out. You might press snooze for fifteen more minutes and feel more rested than if you had gotten up immediately. Either way, you've just enacted the habit, from the cue to the result. Multiply these habits over time, and you've strengthened your neural pathways that shape how you perceive and respond to the world. *What you practice gets stronger.*

Dr. Jud Brewer argues that the results of a habit are the most important thing to focus on, because when we identify negative results of our habits, we're motivated to change them. To unlearn a habit that causes you distress, pain, suffering or discomfort, you can start with the results. You can ask yourself, *What do I get from this habit?* Then you can work your way backwards to understand the habit better, what functions that habit serves, and what alternatives might offer you different results.

At this point, you may be asking, "What do habits have anything to do with Jewish anxiety?" Or you might have already identified a few habits in your life influenced by being, doing, or feeling Jewish. I think Jewish anxiety is a combination of understandable fears and uncertainties about being othered as Jews. But it's not just that. It's also about our inherited, learned, and transmitted habits in how we respond to a world where many of us live in fear and uncertainty about anti-Jewish contempt. It's about how we expose ourselves to Jewish vicarious trauma whenever anything scary happens to other Jews around the world—understandably out of deep concern for our people, but often with terrible costs to our health. We have many habits we've inherited and learned from our ancestors, elders, families and friends that pertain to being, feeling, and doing Jewish in the world. We have many unconscious and automatic habits that play out every day in our lives, in response to inherited trauma, vicarious trauma, and the shame engendered by the assimilation choices of our ancestors. These all result in feeling afraid, unsafe, unworthy, and not accepted. Let's explore those complex experiences now.

Chapter 3

WHY ARE WE SO ANXIOUS? JEWISH TRAUMA, ASSIMILATION, AND SHAME

"Waffling over the expression of identity is probably inherent to all American minority experiences, but it is especially central to, and problematic for, Jewish art, which is often specifically about that waffling and takes its argumentative shape from it too. It was nonetheless shocking to hear, in 2023, what one Broadway insider told me: Mostly we keep quiet because if we talk, they ship us on the trains." One Broadway producer asked me, in the week after the October 7th Hamas attacks: "Have we assimilated too much for people to even see us?" I, too, can't help thinking about the mixed blessing of assimilation, both a goal and a trap. How is it that Jews, in successive waves and for different reasons, keep getting erased from the theatrical culture they did so much to create? Stranger still, they often seem to be holding the eraser, and the scalpel."

—Jesse Green, *New York Times Magazine*,

November 29, 2023[16]

As soon as the Jewish holiday of Purim ends in late winter, I start thinking about the Jewish High Holidays. It's not just about being a planner. It's also a response to collective Jewish anxiety about safety. My organization has no building in which to gather. For the past ten years, we have offered high holiday services in an enormous open tent at the Denver Botanic Gardens on the western edge of a grassy amphitheater bowl where summer concerts take place. The gardens are open to the public: there are no metal detectors or bag checks at the general entrance, and anyone can walk in for free on those days. The tent fits about 1,200 people. The amphitheater, when completely full, can easily accommodate 1,000 people. We offer nine services over Rosh Hashanah and Yom Kippur. That's a lot of Jews and our loved ones in one space.

Truthfully, I always feel a little scared about what might happen to Jews leading into the high holiday season, in a country awash in guns, shootings, political polarization, and anti-Jewish oppression. When we begin planning, I'm not thinking about what I want to explore in my *d'vrei Torah* (sermons) or potential new music to introduce. I'm safety planning and working with our contacts at the Denver police department and the Secure Community Network, a national Jewish non-profit that works on security and safety in Jewish communities. We do intense pre-planning because we are a small team, with no security officers on staff. Every year, we discuss how to balance concerns about potential active shooters with many people's discomfort and fear of armed police officers, especially for Jews of color.

In writing this, I'm noticing tension in my shoulders, my brow has furrowed, and my breathing has become a bit shallower. This embodied tension is a manifestation of Jewish anxiety. It's also a justifiable response to existential questions about our safety in the U.S. in this historical moment.

Our anxiety about safety is a response to violence against Jews throughout Jewish history. We learn how to respond to the fear and uncertainty about the world through deeply anxious family systems. We continue to live with threats of violence against us today. From these anxious, fearful places in ourselves, families, and communities, we respond to the real manifestations of anti-Jewish oppression we experience in a world filled with contempt for, and vitriol against Jews, especially on social media platforms. We don't have to gaslight ourselves that we're just too sensitive or over-reactive. Our Jewish anxiety is real, because we are constantly *othered* with contempt, disgust, hatred, and ignorance.

Our anxious responses to being othered happen on three levels simultaneously. First, our collective traumatic past informs and impinges on our uncertain present. Everything we might have learned or experienced first, second, or third hand intergenerationally show up in our present moments when we feel othered, afraid, uncertain, shamed, or blamed as Jews. Second, and equally powerful, we experience significant stress, fear, and uncertainty, as we move through a world that often expresses outright contempt, hostility, and insidious ambivalence toward us Jews as human beings, worthy of dignity, care, love, respect, and belonging. Third, because our ancestors embraced assimilation as the dominant strategy for belonging in North America, we often feel confused, ambivalent, distressed, or alienated about what being Jewish means to *us.* Sometimes, we just don't know what it means, but we fear being targeted, nonetheless. This ambivalence, confusion, and not-knowing causes us so much stress about whether we're Jewish enough and whether we truly belong in our communities (Jewish and beyond). This stress shows up in our bodies, our perceptions, and our habits as we internalize and metabolize all those experiences that call into question our sense of safety, worth, acceptance, and belonging in the world.

In her powerful book, *We Need to Talk About Antisemitism,* Rabbi Diana Fersko examines how Jewish people are othered.[17] She argues that anti-Jewish oppression is based on conspiracy theories, distortions, and outright lies, and describes how Jews are contemptuously dismissed, dehumanized, and stigmatized as different, foreign, threatening, unwelcome, and unworthy of care. One way this happens is through interpersonal interactions and microaggressions, which Fersko says "are their own type of injury, the everyday papercuts that Jews encounter." These microaggressions include people making intrusive, denigrating, offensive remarks about Jewish hair, bodies, ethnicities, and appearances. They include hostile and aggressive exchanges, especially on social media platforms, where people make assumptions, without empathy or curiosity, about our politics regarding Israel, Gaza, and Palestine, or when the word "Zionist" is contemptuously snarled, with disdain. It's when a sixth grader sees "Jews=murderers" scratched out in her middle school bathroom. It's when my daughter witnessed posters of hostages in Gaza defaced with swastikas and ripped into pieces in the hallway of her high school after the Hamas attacks.

Cultural othering happens when schools blithely schedule important events and tests on major Jewish holidays, even after requests to take those holidays into account. It's when shops, grocery stores, organizations, workplaces, and schools offer tokenizing and empty gestures of diversity for the December holiday season, presuming that Chanukah is as important as Christmas on the holiday calendar (it's not). A few years ago, a local grocery store posted hilarious, yet depressing signs that said "Celebrate Chanukah" advertising the price of ham, with an accompanying large display of matzah, chocolate gelt, and gefilte fish (one out of three is progress?).

Anti-Jewish ignorance, contempt, and oppression influences our choices in how we express ourselves (or not) as Jews. It shows up in our embodied sensations, our thoughts and feelings, our habitual behaviors, our communal conversations. We internalize the world's hatred, ambivalence, contempt, and othering, whether we're conscious of it or not. We learn to feel less safe, welcome, and worthy of care as a minority in a majority culture. Sometimes we feel erased and invisible as Jews. Sometimes, paradoxically, we experience hyper-visibility and fear, because of how we look and/or what we wear that might out us as Jews. And depending on how our other identities weave together with being Jewish, this erasure, invisibility, and hyper-visibility get even more complicated.

Internalizing all this anti-Jewish oppression is an understandable response to a world where our sense of safety, worth, and belonging feels dicey and uncertain. Let me be perfectly clear, lest anyone reading this think I'm engaging in victim-blaming. *I'm not blaming us.* I'm speaking from my own deeply felt, direct lived experience of Jewish anxiety.

THREE TRUTHS THAT CO-EXIST SIMULTANEOUSLY

One: it's not our fault we feel Jewishly anxious. Living in this world is undeniably anxiety-provoking. Two: always presuming we will be victimized, oppressed, and excluded, out of habit, feels terrible. We suffer as a result. Three: we have choices in each moment about how to respond to fear and uncertainty. We are not powerless. Sadly, we often choose repetitive thoughts, feelings, and behaviors to deal with our need for safety, worth, and belonging. Sometimes our habits amplify our suffering. These habits result in making us *more* anxious, not less.

These Jewish anxiety habits spread, like an invisible but powerful social contagion, within our families, our friend circles, and our wider Jewish communities. Our anxiety habits become unconscious, automatic, ingrained, and embodied as tightness and stress. We don't even notice we're reacting anxiously. We think, *That's just how I am, that's just how we are.* We don't realize or pause to consider alternative choices. We react physically, cognitively, emotionally, and behaviorally from that tightened, scared, anxious and sometimes angry place of feeling vulnerable, unsafe, unwelcome, and unworthy of care.

We practice anxiety out of habit because we learn to presume and anticipate being othered. We internalize all this terrible anti-Jewish oppression in ways that habitually constrict our perceptions of reality and shape our responses to the uncertainty of our safety, our worth as human beings, and our belonging.

Our anxiety habits are not immutable. We are adaptable, creative, resilient people. We have the capacity to engage in *tikkun atzmi:* self-transformation and change. We have both suffered greatly and celebrated so many achievements throughout Jewish history. We know from Jewish tradition, particularly from the liturgy of Yom Kippur about *teshuvah* (literally, return and repair): that *internal transformation,* in service of healing relationships with ourselves and with others is possible. Through the insights of neuroscience research, we're also learning just how much our brains are neuroplastic, flexible, and can change through conscious effort and practice. We can learn new things if we adopt a growth mindset and adopt different behaviors. I know from my own life it's possible to help our brains, hearts, and bodies learn how to change our habits, and adapt in response to new experiences, new learning, and new stimuli—if we are open to it. We can unlearn our anxiety habits with concepts, tools, skills, and practice, to learn how to adopt new, different, *and better* habits. I believe that change is possible. We can suffer less.

THIS IS YOUR BRAIN ON INHERITED JEWISH TRAUMA

> "When we don't attend to trauma, it can start to permeate our lives. While we may know that the initial pain can hold our bodies hostage, we often overlook that it refuses to stay within the confines of our singular bodies, that it moves through relationships, within our families, our communities, and across society, multiplying the pain."
>
> **—Prentiss Hemphill, *What It Takes to Heal*[18]**

There's a rich research conversation about the impacts of trauma, and the culturally specific contours of Jewish trauma in particular. These insights can help us untangle the subtle differences between different kinds of trauma and how anxiety can show up as a residual, learned response. One distinction to understand is the differences between traumatic lived experiences, inherited trauma, and vicarious trauma. I'll briefly discuss each of these and how they connect to Jewish history, culture, and habits.

Trauma researcher Dr. Bessel van der Kolk describes in *The Body Keeps the Score* how traumatic events create definitive physiological changes by rewiring our brains.[19] When a person or group of people experience a traumatic event (or series of events over time, which is known as complex PTSD*),* the event(s) typically involve a life-threatening loss of control and generates intense, overwhelming fear about safety. Our brains, nervous systems, and muscles learn how to respond to this threat to safety in real time through fight, flight, freeze, and/or fawn strategies, to ensure our survival.

These traumatic memories re-activate when we experience a present moment cue, that reminds us (whether consciously or unconsciously) of our embodied past trauma and triggers an overwhelming fear of loss of control. This re-activation of our nervous system's stress response feels particularly acute when we feel physically and/or emotionally unsafe. The past infringes on the present, and short-circuits our nervous system into survival mode, *even when the cue or trigger is not life-threatening*. When this happens, we're responding from our amygdala, not our pre-frontal cortex, and our vision is narrowed. We respond with hyper-vigilance and hyper-arousal. This trauma response then compromises our ability to respond to what is happening in the present moment when our lives are not necessarily threatened. Traumatic experiences impair our ability to concentrate, emotionally self-regulate, and form trusting relationships. Over time, our bodies experience repetitive floods of stress hormones that impair our immune systems and organ function.

What happens when an entire group of people experience collective trauma? In *Trauma and Recovery: The Aftermath of Violence, from Domestic Abuse to Political Terror,* psychiatrist Dr. Judith Herman, the eldest child of two secular Jewish Eastern European parents, writes about how trauma is not just personal or interpersonal, it's political.[20] Trauma happens at the interpersonal level within couples and families, and between groups with asymmetrical power. When a dominant group abuses power against another group, the less powerful group experiences stigma, marginalization, oppression, physical violence, terror, and death. Journalist Isabel Wilkerson, in her influential book, *Caste: The Origins of Our Discontents,* describes the ways powerful groups (such as Brahmins in India, white people in the United States, and Nazis in the Third Reich) have deployed social hierarchies, customs, law, and state violence to collectively and contemptuously traumatize less powerful groups, such as the Dalits, Black Americans, and Jews.[21] This constant othering, baked into the structure of cultures, leaves long-lasting traumatic effects that are passed down intergenerationally. How does it apply to contemporary American Jews?

REMEMBERING JEWISH TRAUMA THROUGH RITUAL AND CULTURE

Jewish tradition and observance can encourage my anxiety in a way that sometimes is not helpful. Since I've become observant, Passover cleaning can bring up anxiety. The build-up to Shabbat can be anxiety-provoking. I know that my practices can sometimes teeter into anxiety. And non-Jewish people

"We were slaves in Egypt, living under the oppression of Pharoah." "Never forget, never again." Jews retell and re-enact traumatic narratives, myths, and lived experiences throughout the year in our cultural and religious rituals, such as the Passover Seder, reading the Book of Esther for Purim, and the Book of Lamentations on Tisha B'Av (commemorating the

never even think about these things! My grandparents used to say, "The goyim (non-Jews) have a restful tuches (bottom) in the way that Jews don't." They don't have to worry about the things we have to do and prepare for the holidays. It's a quality of restlessness and uneasiness—but it also drives our creativity, and why we've excelled in certain fields, where it's rewarded. But there's such a cost to that restlessness.

—Moshe, thirties

destruction of the First and Second Temples in Jerusalem). We are exhorted to remember our difficult history of oppression through Jewish liturgy, movies, books, plays, museum exhibitions, and podcasts. We remember and teach our children about traumatic loss in Jewish museums, public memorials, and ceremonies, especially to remember the millions of Jews persecuted and murdered in the Holocaust.

These memories, cultural practices, rituals, and stories live inside us as formative narratives, myths, and learned behavioral habits about our own safety, worth, and belonging in the world, in the present moment. Our cultural practices are relevant because they influence the blurry line between Jewish inherited trauma, cultural/religious traditions, and learned anxiety habits.

THE JEWISH HISTORY DOUBLE HELIX: TRAUMA AND RESILIENCE

Think of Jewish history as a double helix strand of DNA. One strand of that double helix is the unassailable truth that our people have endured multiple experiences of anti-Jewish collective trauma over the past two millennia, from forced conversions, conquests, expulsions, displacements, disenfranchisement, and genocide. In 1963, Professor Salo Baron named this as "the lachrymose narrative of Jewish history."[22] However, less than two decades after the Holocaust, Baron boldly urged Jewish Studies scholars to move away from this lopsided perspective of history that overemphasized persecution and suffering. This was a tough sell, given the historical circumstances. Jews were only beginning to process the scale, degree, and profound impact of collective Jewish trauma in Europe at that time. Over the past sixty years, Jewish history scholars have subsequently debated the question of whether, and to what degree, suffering from anti-Jewish oppression should inhabit the center of Jewish historical analysis. The debate will not end any time soon.

The second strand of Jewish history's double helix is that Jews have creatively adapted to difficult, uncertain, and sometimes traumatic circumstances with resilience and fortitude. Jews have enlisted ingenuity, persistence, and creativity to shape, adapt, re-invent, survive and thrive in Jewish communities, across places, spaces, and historical eras. In the monumental, three volume work, *Cultures of the Jews: A New History,* edited by David Biale, scholars show how Jews throughout history have always created distinctive, autonomous cultural forms, in conversation with the places and cultures where Jews have lived.[23] In Hebrew, the expression *gam v' gam* means both/and. Creativity *and* uncertainty. Resilience *and* oppression. Both these strands of the Jewish double helix of history are true and necessary to understand how Jews grapple with inherited and intergenerational trauma.

WHAT IS INHERITED, INTERGENERATIONAL JEWISH TRAUMA?

> *Nobody taught me that we have a choice about being anxious. It becomes an ingrained environmental response, because it was actively taught to me to be anxious about everything in life. Always have a passport and a suitcase to flee, just in case.*
>
> **—Nina, fifties**

Trauma scholars Dr. Rachel Yehuda and Amy Lehrner define intergenerational trauma as "exposure to extremely adverse events [which] impacts individuals to such a great extent that their offspring find themselves grappling with their parents' post-traumatic state."[24] After World War II, researchers began to explore intergenerational

I found a book that my grandma wrote for me when I was born, she fled from Germany. It has the names of my great-grandmothers that I didn't know. Because of our trauma, there's so much silence and so many gaps in my knowing, because not much was said. I feel like that journey is just starting.
—Mari, forties

trauma emerged in response to the psychological distress of Holocaust survivors and their families. One important finding from this body of research is that the children and grandchildren of Holocaust survivors experience their own form of inherited, intergenerational trauma, by living with and witnessing the symptoms and behaviors of their parents and grandparents, even if they never learn what happened "over there."

Rabbi Tirzah Firestone's life experience as the daughter of a survivor aligns with this research insight. In her recent *Wounds into Wisdom: Healing Intergenerational Jewish Trauma,* she argues that the unhealed pain and traumatic responses of family members, coupled with the silences of untold family stories, become the strongest influences in transmitting Jewish ancestral trauma. We might not know about our elders' or ancestors' direct experience of their traumatic past, but we learn it unconsciously by watching how *they* respond to the world in constricted, fearful ways that are never explicitly acknowledged or named as trauma responses. She writes:

> I am a second-generation Holocaust survivor. My mother escaped Nazi Germany in 1939, leaving behind scores of relatives who were murdered in unconscionable ways. Even though she never spoke of them, I felt the reverberations of the family's unprocessed shock, grief, and trauma. Ultimately, this led me to uncover the family history and then as a rabbi and psychotherapist, to study the effects of collective trauma in my people and far beyond.[25]

Today, every time a traumatic event occurs in the world against Jews, a shock wave reverberates through the local and global community, with ripple effects for generations. For example, I went to Argentina in 2025 on a Jewish cultural trip. Our hotel was a block from the former Israeli Embassy in Buenos Aires, which is now a memorial park. Before our trip ended, the police began setting up enormous, seven-foot tall, black metal barriers all along the street. Why? Because in 1994, the Israeli Embassy and the Jewish Community Center in Buenos Aires were bombed within months of one another, and the anniversary of that trauma was coming up. Thirty years later, and most likely for many decades to come, these painful, terrifying anniversaries will be commemorated by the Buenos Aires Jewish community and will shape the collective memory of children born long afterwards.

Similarly, for North American Jews across the political spectrum, we live with the memory of the attacks in Israel on October 7, 2023, the traumatic experiences of hostages, and the devastating war in Gaza. This contemporary example has created vast, traumatic ripple effects throughout the world. We are only at the initial cusp of beginning to understand and process the reverberating psychological and moral implications of this profound collective trauma, which will influence the lives of subsequent generations of Israelis, Palestinians, and Jews around the world for decades to come.[26]

THE PAST INTRUDES ON THE PRESENT

Even when we're safe and not at all threatened by the prospect of violence, our inherited trauma shapes us and creates suffering in the present moment, within ourselves and our families. It deforms how we respond to the present when we're triggered by a discomfiting cue about our past, and then we react unconsciously with fight, flight, freeze, and fawn, even though we are safe, loved, and accepted as Jews in that moment of reaction.

Here's a personal story. My former partner was raised in a devout Catholic family and has enthusiastically raised our daughter Jewishly for eighteen years. About fourteen years ago, she excitedly brought home a flyer from her job in public service and said, "Let's participate in this as a family!" I looked at the flyer and recoiled. The headline was "Annual Christmas Crusade!" The bottom of the page featured a Christmas tree, festive wreaths, and a pile of toys. Apparently, for the past thirty years, Denver law enforcement has organized a winter gift drive for children in need. No doubt, this was a lovely holiday effort to show love and care for kids.

But my response? I became absolutely apoplectic. My inherited Jewish trauma response prompted a raging blowout. I railed against the nomenclature of the event. My former partner was hurt and angered that I was so hung up on the name, I could not see its worth. She felt bewildered that I was lambasting something she loved and participated in every year. After many years of reflection, I can now say that I was, as therapist Terrence Real would say "offending from the victim position": attacking the event because of my own Jewish inherited trauma.

Here were some of the bombs I lobbed: Christmas Crusade? How could public agencies use the language of *crusade?* What happened to the separation of religion and state? Did anyone understand how upsetting that word might be for Jewish and Muslim employees, whose ancestors were targeted in Christian Crusade holy wars from 1095-1291 across Europe and the Middle East? What about all the other city employees who might otherwise want to participate in a gesture of generosity, but felt similarly excluded by the explicitly Christian language of this? Does anyone in city government have awareness of exercising Christian privilege? Phew.

I picked epic, annual fights about language, Christian

obliviousness, privilege, and hegemony. I tried to convey what it felt like for me to navigate the tsunami of complicated Jewish feelings every December. I couldn't articulate then what I know now to be a cascade of fight and flight responses: learned Jewish habits of feeling victimized, moving into defensiveness, agitation, and attack. I felt misunderstood, frustrated, and deeply *alone*. My former partner simply could not understand why I felt so offended and attacked, nor could she understand why I was attacking *her*. She felt misunderstood, frustrated, and deeply alone. It wasn't until she said, "Don't shoot your ally" that I could hear her. From her perspective, this wasn't about me or about Jews, it was about helping vulnerable kids. *Yes, and.* We were arguing about content and history, but I was responding from intense, intergenerational trauma habits. And holy wow, did this result in great cost to our relationship and my own nervous system.

In hindsight, I recognize how much this impacted my body for years. I experienced back spasms, tightness in my neck, and insomnia. I remember a couple of nights where I was up at 3am, speechifying in righteous indignation to all the well-meaning Christians in the world, silently pontificating about how nice it must feel to be utterly oblivious about religious diversity. After several years, I realized this pattern felt awful. I tried to find an alternative. I begrudgingly agreed to participate. *But only* if we agreed to reframe this whole enterprise as a "winter holiday *mitzvah* project" (*mitzvah* = actions, grounded in values, that show we care about an important relationship). I can see more clearly now how my own re-enactment of inherited Jewish trauma harmed me. It harms our beloveds, our best allies, our families, and our communities.

The ripple effects of inherited, intergenerational Jewish trauma live in our bodies as sensations tightness, stress, contraction, and adrenaline. Our Jewish anxiety lingers in our muscles and fascia. This inheritance shapes our unconscious feelings, behaviors, and our souls. We attack, retreat, get overly busy, go numb, or try to people please. When we don't acknowledge and attend to our inherited Jewish trauma responses with care and compassion, our present moment becomes fueled by Jewish anxiety habits as residue from the past. And we imprint the effects of Jewish inherited trauma onto future generations, like a haunted, ghostly presence.

VICARIOUS TRAUMA: OVEREXPOSING OURSELVES TO JEWISH SUFFERING

Vicarious trauma forms another piece of the Jewish anxiety puzzle. The concept was first developed in the 1980s by therapists Irene Lisa McCann and Laurie Anne Pearlman to address the challenges of working with trauma survivors, and how constant exposure to other people's trauma can adversely impact helping professionals. Vicarious trauma exposure can lead to symptoms of post-traumatic stress disorder, such as avoidance, numbness, hypervigilance, and hyperarousal. Studies have found that vicarious trauma can also increase stress, anxiety, and burnout.[27] Three components of vicarious trauma are relevant to understanding our Jewish anxiety habits: empathic engagement and exposure to graphic, traumatizing material and narratives; exposure to the impact of human cruelty; and the re-enactment of trauma in ordinary situations that are not actually traumatic.

I think this concept has deep resonance for Jews, because we unwittingly expose ourselves to Jewish vicarious trauma all the time. This is understandable. As a global people, we care deeply about what happens to other Jews around the world. We justifiably worry about how the impact of anti-Jewish contempt and violence elsewhere might create harm toward us locally. On the one hand, I appreciate this expression of communal connection and concern. But on the other hand, it's far too easy to overexpose ourselves and experience Jewish vicarious trauma. It's easier to suffer from vicarious trauma today, because of the speed at which media globally ricochets in a twenty-four-hour news cycle, and because of our doomscrolling and media consumption habits. We voraciously consume media to feel connected, informed, and to stave off feelings of powerlessness and loss of control. We tell ourselves this is how we can feel more empowered, connected to other Jews and in control of our lives. But some of the results of these habits are profoundly negative: we wind up *amplifying* our anxieties, and we exacerbate our fears.

What do we get from these overexposure and oversaturation habits? It's complicated and not clear-cut. Some of us decide to donate money to help others who are suffering (a worthy mitzvah to show our care). Some of us organize and attend vigils to mourn and feel connected, to stave off feeling isolated and scared. Some of us hop onto planes to witness and attend to the trauma of others in need. Some of us freeze and go numb. After the October 7th attacks, we grieved deeply, suffering from insomnia, agitation, fear, anger, and despair. Our Jewish vicarious trauma has cumulative, harmful, lasting effects in our bodies and our perception of Jewish safety, worth and belonging in the world.

We also expose ourselves and our children to Jewish vicarious trauma through how we teach Jewish history and culture, how we talk about violence against Jews, and through heritage tours that center the Holocaust. Here are just two of many personal examples in my family.

In 1985, when I was sixteen years old, my synagogue's high school program screened Claude Lanzmann's *The Shoah*, a nine-hour documentary of first-person testimonies of survivors, former Nazis, witnesses, and bystanders. After screening the film over two Sunday afternoons in four and a half hour chunks, students split into small groups after each screening to process what we had just experienced. After each screening, I felt completely disassociated, frozen, and numb. I didn't have the language for those feelings at the time. I couldn't speak; I was so saturated with overwhelm and fear. I walked away feeling shaken, scared, and profoundly unsafe as a Jew in the world. I assumed the worst—that this horror might happen again. This formed my sense that we Jews were, are, and will be victims, first and foremost. I doubt this was the goal of my well-meaning Jewish educators, but it's what I walked away with, nonetheless.

Thirty-eight years later, my sixteen-year-old daughter Sasha participated in a five-week trip to Poland and Israel through the local Jewish Federation. They visited Polish synagogues and learned a bit about the rich Jewish history of the region, where my grandfather lived, and from where our family traces our ancestry back to the early 1770s. They also visited sites of anti-Jewish oppression, suffering, and death: Treblinka, Majdanek, and Auschwitz-Birkenau. Sasha called me after those visits, shaken and deeply distressed. She said, "Ima, if I had been born seventy-five years ago, if great-grandpa George [my grandfather] had not left Warsaw, that could have been me."

Yes/and, *gam v'gam*. What are the goals and messages about Jewish history, memory, identity and community we want to convey? That our children now might become victims in the future? I understand the importance of teaching Jewish history, in all its complexity, to emerging generations of Jews. But to return to the double helix metaphor of Jewish trauma *and* resilience, what do we get—what are the results—when we habitually subject ourselves and our children to Jewish inherited and vicarious trauma, by over-emphasizing our lachrymose history of victimization, suffering, trauma, and death, at the expense of learning about our collective resilience and creative adaptation? We get Jewishly anxious.

Here is another example of extreme Jewish vicarious trauma: after the October 7th Hamas attacks in Israel, the IDF (Israel Defense Forces) compiled a forty-seven-minute film of raw footage, including footage from body cameras worn by Hamas terrorists. The film, officially called *Bearing Witness*, is informally called "The Atrocities Film" in Hebrew. Full disclaimer: I have not, cannot, and will not see this film. I already suffer from too much vicarious Jewish trauma and overexposure after October 7th, and I know my nervous system would not be able to handle it. However, I can say with confidence that to view this reality-horror film qualifies as Jewish vicarious trauma exposure, due to its gruesome, violent nature. Watching the film involves empathic engagement with the terror, suffering, and murder of victims in the attacks. The viewer is exposed to extremely graphic, murder, mutilation, beheading, and other profoundly upsetting material. I can only imagine how traumatized the IDF soldiers who compiled the film are. I can only imagine how viewers walked away from that film, and how viewing that footage has subsequently affected them. You cannot unsee images of such brutality and horror afterwards.

What are the cumulative effects of all of this inherited and vicarious trauma? Our anxiety manifests in the form of *internalizing* and *metabolizing* anti-Jewish oppression as a primary and core aspect of our identity. We perceive ourselves as victims first and foremost. We create and enact deeply grooved, maladaptive habits as a response. We learn to assume a lack of safety. We learn to assume, fear, and prepare for the possibility that collective trauma and the abuse of power could easily happen again. We learn to catastrophize because, if we look to Jewish history and our recent past, the worst possible things have already happened. We learn to question whether we are inherently worthy of love, care, and respect. We question whether we truly belong in our own skin, in our communities and in the world. We presume that we won't or don't belong, unless we fawn, hide, minimize, or shrink who we really are. We learn to presume exclusion, not welcome. We reproduce and transmit aspects of that inherited Jewish trauma, internalized oppression, and learned anxiety in our relationships, within our families and communities. We project our fears about safety, worth, and belonging onto other Jews who are "not like us," which triggers threat responses. We attack and defend from that sense of perceived threat. We also project those fears onto people in our lives who are not Jewish, but who are often our best and closest allies, who love us and are not out to get us or dilute our Jewishness. This keeps our nervous systems constantly on high arousal. It makes us defensive and requires hypervigilance. It's utterly exhausting.

ASSIMILATION AND INTERNALIZED SHAME

I've always worried: have I studied hard enough? Did I get good enough grades? Did the teacher like me enough, will I find a boyfriend? It went on to worry about my body being too big, am I pretty enough? The Jewish part is that I didn't have hair like the other girls, I had frizzy Jewish curly hair. I wish I had accepted it, but I always struggled to straighten it and fight against it, I always wanted to fit in.

—Carly, fifties

There's one more piece to understanding Jewish anxiety: the unintended legacy of assimilation. Today, this legacy looks, sounds, and feels like internalized Jewish shame. We habitually think we are not enough.

Dr. Brené Brown defines shame as "the intensely painful feeling or experience of believing that we are flawed and therefore unworthy of love and belonging—something we've experienced, done, or failed to do makes us unworthy of connection."[28] Internalized Jewish shame is anti-Jewish contempt turned inwards on ourselves. It shows up in our repetitive thoughts, feelings, and behaviors suggesting that we are not okay as we are, we're not enough Jewishly, and, even more pernicious, that we're bad Jews or bad people, unworthy of care and respect, unworthy of inclusion and belonging.

When some of our Jewish ancestors arrived in the United States (whether prior to, during, or after the mass migration of two and a half million Ashkenazi Jews in the 1880s), they were compelled to navigate a challenging and terrifying system of American white supremacy and a racial caste system. This encounter with racial hierarchy and inequality required Jews to adapt for survival. Historically, Jewish inclusion in the United States has depended on conforming to racial mores that both brutally subjugated African Americans and encouraged Jews shed their identification with Jewish distinctiveness. If possible, given one's skin color, Jews felt pressure to embrace assimilation into whiteness, because they saw the conditional benefits that whiteness offered. Jo Kent Katz, author of *Transcending Jewish Trauma*, writes:

> We may not be aware of the political conditions or specific circumstances that informed our families' immigration or their early experiences of assimilation. Thus, our thoughts, feelings, and behaviors may be decontextualized, deeply informed by experiences to which we have no conscious connection.[29]

For Ashkenazi Jews, the late nineteenth-century racial discourse at the time viewed Jews as inferior, inhabiting a lower rung than white, Anglo-Saxon Protestants. Eric Goldstein, in *The Price of Whiteness: Jews, Race, and American Identity,* writes about how Ashkenazi Jews with lighter skin were considered conditionally more acceptable and superior to Black Americans. Because Ashkenazi Jews embraced this racial and political project of assimilation with wholehearted enthusiasm, they were not primarily seen as a threat to the existing racial hierarchy. But embracing that racial hierarchy came with its own costs, which still reverberate a century later in Jewish uncertainty, ambivalence, confusion, alienation, and simply not knowing what being Jewish could mean today.[30]

Here's an example: the first talkie film ever made, in 1927, was *The Jazz Singer*. The son of religious Ashkenazi Jewish immigrants tries to make it in jazz music by rejecting his father's plea to become a cantor. He changes his name and plays piano in black face. The central conflict of the film asks the question of whether it's possible to live fully as a Jew *and* fully immersed in a white supremacist American society, rather than always feeling, as Adrienne Rich described, "split at the root."[31] For much of the twentieth century, much of Ashkenazi Jewish cultural production (in novels, plays, movies, and music), involved the expression of deep longing to be accepted in American society. And in America, that has always meant making a complex bargain with white supremacy.

This centuries-long assimilation project was a complicated "mixed blessing," as Jesse White wrote in the quote at the beginning of this chapter. It was both a goal and trap, for those with lighter skin, and it has never been available to Jews of color with darker skin. I understand why Ashkenazi ancestors embraced the goal of wanting to be safe, seen, and accepted. My own grandfather wholeheartedly embraced this by changing his name from Yossl Leibl Itzkowitz to George Louis. But in this moment of Jewish history, I've come to think that the outcomes of this project are indeed a trap. April Rosenblum, in *The Past Didn't Go Anywhere,* writes:

> Many oppressions rely on keeping a targeted group of people poor, uneducated, designated non-white, or otherwise "at the bottom." Anti-Jewish oppression doesn't depend on that. Although at many times it has kept Jews in poverty or designated non-white, these have been "optional" features. Because the point of anti-Jewish oppression is to keep a Jewish face in front, so that Jews, instead of ruling classes, become the target for peoples' rage, it works even more smoothly when Jews are allowed some success and can be perceived as the ones "in charge" by other oppressed groups.[32]

And during periodic, undulating waves of pernicious anti-Jewish stereotypes, rhetoric, and violence that circulate in American culture, such as the time we're living through now, post-October 7th and the war in Gaza, we feel urgently anxious. Our sense of safety and belonging feel uncertain and unstable because of the rise in overt anti-Jewish and anti-Israel sentiment. For Jews who have critiqued the widespread destruction and death in Gaza, our sense of worth and belonging *in our own Jewish* communities feels uncertain and unstable. This is the reality of being othered by anti-Jewish oppression, despite our ancestors' best efforts to blend in.

Although our ancestors would never have predicted, nor would they have wanted us to feel anxious about our places in society, the assimilation project has created many doubts in our minds about whether we're worthy, enough, or whether we truly belong as Jews. And we feel ashamed about this experience, but we almost never talk about it. Our internalized shame simply drives our anxiety habits. I will explore what Jewish internalized shame habits look like much more in the next chapter. But as a sneak preview, here are what some Jewish shame statements sound like: beginning conversations with headlines of who we aren't, and how what we don't do Jewish makes us bad Jews. When people talk with me, no matter how old or young, how they grew up, or what they do now, many people lead with habitual fear and vulnerability of being inadequate Jewishly. What I hear all the time: "I'm a bad Jew because I don't know Hebrew… I don't believe in God… I don't keep kosher… I love bacon and cheeseburgers… I love someone who is not Jewish… I don't belong to or ever go to a synagogue… I put up a Christmas tree… I don't know anything about Shabbat…" and on and on. If you've ever said anything like this or you find yourself nodding in recognition, the next chapter will dive deeply into how internalized Jewish shame habits are not our fault. We can change them.

How we choose to respond to the stress of anti-Jewish oppression, and care for ourselves, is what makes all the difference. We suffer terribly when we respond to stress without awareness or self-compassion. Our learned and transmitted habits of responding to the stress of being Jewish in the world, and internalizing all that oppression, is to respond with fight/flight/freeze/fawn habits. The next chapter explores three common Jewish anxiety stress responses to being othered. These habits revolve around existential fears about our safety; our uncertainty about whether we're worthy of love, care and respect; and our deeply felt human needs for acceptance and belonging. All these habits are understandable. We can change them with *tikkun atzmi:* caring for ourselves with awareness, kindness, compassion, and practice. We'll explore how to map our anxiety habits by returning to the habit loop and identify when we're triggered, what's happening in our bodies, what we're thinking and feeling, and what we need in those difficult moments. Once we have a clear sense of what we need, we can discern what behavioral alternatives we might choose to create different results—and less anxiety.

Chapter 4

SAFETY, WORTH, AND BELONGING

I feel like it's [anti-Jewish sentiment] almost constant. Other than the ordinary microaggressions of ignorance and cultural normativity, I've "only" had two hate incidents. One was online this year, and the other was back in California, in the progressive bubble. I was wearing a kippah, and someone came up to me and commented with hate in their voice, "Are you Jewish? I hate Jews." I was startled and scared.

—Izzy, forties

Now that we've explored insights of neuroscience, and the different ways anti-Jewish oppression causes us harm, it's time to examine how we can apply these ideas to our lived experience. Let's go back to the anxiety equation: fear + uncertainty + our habits.

Our habitual responses to fear and uncertainty carve neural grooves that often unwittingly increase our distress. Here I want to explore common anxiety habits we develop in response to our fears and uncertainties about our safety, our inherent worthiness, and our yearning for belonging and acceptance. When we experience anti-Jewish othering, oppression, and contempt, all these fears and uncertainties get activated in our nervous systems, and we tend to respond in ways that amplify, rather than alleviate, our fears.

Here are some questions we'll explore: how might our responses *aggravate,* rather than soothe, our inherited and vicarious trauma? How do we internalize anti-Jewish oppression, by turning that contempt inwards toward ourselves in the form of shame? How do we sometimes project it outwards against other Jews and people we perceive as potential threats, when in fact, they might be our allies?

This is an opportunity to explore your own habits. In each section, I'll invite you to map out your own patterns, using the clock metaphor from chapter one to look for your own anxiety cues, sensations, feelings, thoughts, needs, behaviors, and results. I'll offer prompt questions so that you can explore how different triggers cue your anxiety habit loops. These exercises can help you assess the results of your habits, and whether they increase or decrease anxiety in your body, thoughts, and feelings.

The big questions to consider as you read this chapter: what do I get from my fear, control, avoidance, distraction, and internal shaming habits? What are the results of responding to uncertainty from my/our inherited and vicarious trauma habits? Does a particular habit meet my need for safety? Do any of my habits of feelings, thoughts, and actions affirm what I need, or do my habits undermine my sense of inherent worth and dignity? Does a particular habit I have around the need to belong *contribute* to my sense of acceptance and belonging in the world, or does it amplify my thoughts and feelings of aloneness and exclusion?

How do my habits show up in my body as tightness and contraction? Do my habits help me feel calm, secure, and emotionally self-regulated? If your answers to these questions are sometimes or consistently no, that's an important insight and a moment of potential transformation. If you can create more awareness about your habits, and most importantly, your awareness about the results of your habits, you can begin to identify and make different choices that might better meet your own needs. Making different choices that offer better alternatives is what we'll explore in the following chapters of the book.

My hope is that this chapter offers you descriptive examples, specific tools, and gentle, compassionate questions to begin to see more clearly when, where, and how you fall into a Jewish anxiety habit hole, and to know that you're not alone. Once you can identify your patterns, you can assess what habits you want to change, and how to change them, to suffer less and feel more relief.

There are also wider communal implications here. When you start to see your own Jewish anxiety habits, you'll probably notice that many Jews have similar anxiety responses to anti-Jewish oppression. You might begin to be aware of how you learned these habits by watching friends, family members, and folks in your community respond to Jewish fears and uncertainties in habitual ways. Jewish anxiety is *social:* our anxieties create ripple effects among individuals, our families, and our wider communities. In other words, it's not just you—it's us, in how we as a people respond to anti-Jewish oppression and the challenges of being othered in difficult and uncertain world.

The Talmud (Sanhedrin 37a), teaches "anyone who sustains one soul from the Jewish people, it's as if they sustained an entire world."[33] To extend the metaphor, if you can identify your habit, and choose differently to nourish and sustain your own soul by choosing different responses to fear and uncertainty, you can change your world. Collectively, if we can identify our communal habits that increase, rather than decrease, our suffering from anxiety, we can change the entire world and suffer less.

SAFETY AND OTHERING: RESPONDING TO FEAR AND UNCERTAINTY

In 1987, my parents dropped me off at Indiana University, where I was planning to study opera. On move-in day, I met my roommate Nicki, who was from Martinsville, Indiana. She was white, had bouncy, blond hair, blue eyes, and very fair skin. She had been a high school cheerleader. From the moment we met, she seemed very uncomfortable, as was I. We couldn't have been more different. But I didn't have the language for my discomfort.

I had just returned from Israel and my skin was deep olive and freckled. Nicki remarked on my skin color, my long, textured curly black hair. She noticed and commented on my Star of David necklace, my Israeli leather sandals, and my *Save Soviet Jewry* T-shirt (what can I say, it was the late '80s!). My discomfort grew: her scrutiny and comments felt intrusive and rude. She asked, slowly and incredulously, with a southern Indiana twang, "Wait, are you Jewish?" Why, uhm, yes—yes indeed I am. She looked a little shocked and disclosed that she had never met a real Jew before. She fearfully asked if I had horns, because her daddy told her Jews have horns. I soon learned her father was the grand dragon of the Ku Klux Klan in Indiana. I froze. I tried to be polite, but inside, I felt shocked and scared. I had no idea how to respond. I laughed it off, which I now recognize as fawning, a form of people-pleasing to not rock the boat. I told myself that everything would be fine.

I didn't sleep very well that first week of school, and it wasn't about missing my parents. I couldn't fully relax, and I felt emotionally unsafe. Nicki moved out within a week. I later learned from the RA, not surprisingly, that she didn't feel comfortable living with a Jew.

JEWISH SAFETY FEARS

> *I feel like my anxiety (about safety) is a constant presence. I grew up in Israel, my daughter lives in Israel, I have family there. Growing up there, I learned to look under a bus seat because it could blow up.*
>
> **—Leora, sixties**

Feeling existentially unsafe and afraid is perhaps the most deeply pernicious result of all anti-Jewish oppression. This is a root source of our Jewish anxiety habits, and it's understandable, given our complex, traumatic experiences of contemptuous violence against Jews. In this chapter of Jewish

This is a complicated time to be Jewish and Jewishly anxious. I have friends and family who are freaked out about antisemitism and feel scared that people are coming for them.

—Nina, fifties

Since October 7th, I kept myself separate from the Jewish community, which is not me in other areas of my life. I didn't feel like I had the right to celebrate Jewish holidays. Part of it was "how can I be celebrating when my people are suffering?" What helped me from the beginning was "we survived!" The idea of miracles kept me going, but Passover was hard this year. I was also scared to congregate with other Jews since October 7th.

—Shoshana, forties

history, many of us feel as if the whole world is against us as Jews, from the political right to the political left. These feelings have been exacerbated by our diverse perspectives and relationships to Israel, Zionism, and the war in Gaza. We wonder who we can trust, whether we're emotionally safe, and whether we'll be treated with respect and dignity. It's also why we constantly feel a sense of worry and dread about the present and future—when will we be othered again, and by whom? When will we know it's time to leave for another country? For whom is this option even possible?

When we don't feel safe in our bodies, our homes, our workplaces, on the streets, and in our wider communities, how can we function effectively? When can we exhale and relax? If we always feel scared about potential othering and violence, how can we live freely, without fear? Feeling Jewishly unsafe creates hyper-arousal and hyper-vigilance patterns that get lodged in our bodies as sensations of tightness, contraction, tension, and stress. It re-animates our inherited, intergenerational Jewish trauma. We worry, freeze, get busy to avoid the fear, and try to plan our way out. We fret that there is no truly safe place for us.

One typical Jewish anxiety habit is to ask ourselves, *What's the worst thing that could happen?* when we feel scared. This is understandable, because in the last century, the worst things have already happened to our people, and we still live with the reverberating, generational inherited trauma of the Holocaust. It's an example of our collective past intruding on the present, when the present moment is not necessarily as catastrophic as we might fear. We automatically assume that whatever we're facing in the present moment, the situation warrants catastrophic thinking and strategizing, whether it indeed qualifies as a catastrophe or not.

However, immediately jumping to thoughts about the worst possible outcome, and imagining an apocalyptic future constrains our ability to perceive different responses. We're activated into fight, flight, freeze, or fawn. When we're afraid, we catapult into the future that has not yet arrived, and we miss what's happening in the present moment, especially in our bodies, which grow tighter and more contracted with fear. We fall into a deep habit hole of incessant what-if thinking, which exacerbates those fears. Some of us close ranks by choosing to only associate with other Jews, because that feels safer and more familiar. Some of us habitually try to plan our way out of doomsday scenarios that have not yet, and might not, even happen. For example, with the rightward shift in national and global politics, many Jews now voice collective fears about living through a reprisal of Germany in the 1930s. I know of friends and colleagues who have decided to move to Canada, to update their wills and, for those with European ancestors, have applied for EU passports, "just in case."

When we perceive threat or the real experience of anti-Jewish othering, it knocks out our capacity to use our pre-frontal cortex and kicks us into our individual and communal amygdala. We're in survival mode, navigating our fears and uncertainty about our loss of control. Some of us habitually respond with fight mode strategies (like buying and learning how to shoot a gun), some of us want to flee (packing the suitcase and passport), and some of us go numb and freeze. Some of us engage in fawning strategies (trying to appease people with more power), by blending in, hiding, not wanting to draw attention to ourselves as Jews, and keeping our heads down. Whatever our strategy might be, we become activated to urgently *do something,* anything to deal with the discomfort, fear, and uncertainty of being and feeling othered.

I have observed, in myself and many people I know, the behavior of obsessively checking the news and doomscrolling in response to feeling afraid. These strategies are an attempt to regain a sense of control, because the world can feel so out of control. We unconsciously think *If I know everything about what's happening, and I read every article or news report, I'll be ok.* But when we do this, we habitually oversaturate ourselves with Jewish vicarious trauma. This habit became particularly acute in the days, weeks, and months, and years after October 7th.

Every Jewish person I interviewed for this book said their anxiety dramatically has increased since those attacks. My pastoral counseling load tripled, and my clergy colleagues reported similar observations. For months, I needed to take a couple hours every Shabbat afternoon to simply grieve and cry on the couch to process my own vicarious trauma and empty out the exhaustion of holding space for my community.

Then, when anti-Israel war protests broke out across the country on college campuses in the spring of 2024, some of the explicitly anti-Jewish rhetoric on the left felt shocking to many Jews. This only aggravated our fears about safety, belonging and acceptance. Nina, in her fifties, who identifies as politically progressive, said:

> October 7th and the aftermath [with the war in Gaza and college protest] has really shaken me up. Especially the pain of how younger people and students on campus have reacted. There were protests on my son's college campus. I walked around campus and saw flyers that said, "Israel murdered this person," and nothing at all about the hostages. I'm not a right-winger, but this felt really scary to me, and my son didn't feel scared at all. I think it's

> generational, and the whole framework and online, his professors are all extremely anti-Israel. If you can find a problem, it's Israel, and it gets blurry with anti-Jewish rhetoric. Part of the issue was that I had no control over what he's seeing, and it's dipping into antisemitic stuff. The scary tropes that I see where I just feel like I'm on a weird narrow bridge. I sometimes worry about my kids; they're not going to understand their history.

Indeed, Franklin Foer, in an influential essay published in April 2024, soberly argued that the Golden Age of American Jews, who had enthusiastically supported liberal causes for the last century, is ending.[34] With the rise in overt anti-Jewish contempt online and in the streets, Jews are living through a time of deep anguish, distress, vicarious trauma, pain, fear, and heightened anxiety, with a clearly demarcated before and after rupture in Jewish time since the Hamas attacks and the devastating Israeli military war in Gaza.

In times of crisis, we fear abandonment. We ask ourselves, *Who can I count on for support and back-up?* At clergy meetings in the fall of 2023 after the Hamas attacks, my rabbinic and cantorial colleagues asked in anguish, "Who are our allies in the interfaith community? Why haven't my interfaith clergy friends called me to support us in this terrible time of need?" It can feel lonely in moments of collective fear about our safety. In the spring of 2024, during the college campus protest upheavals, Dalia, in her forties, told me in an interview,

> I have decided to NOT have conversations about how I feel about the Hamas attacks and the war in Gaza with non-Jewish friends at this point. They don't actively hate Jews, but they internalize this idea that we're just white people and they say, "BUT GAZA." And they don't understand how being

> Jewish is not just being white. I've gotten a lot of but, but, but and I hear that I'm not going to be listened to, and it doesn't feel safe. My friends are not willing to entertain that our experiences in the world differ because we're Jewish.

Here are some Jewish worry questions about safety I've heard over the years. How many of these have you asked as well? *What if someone comes to our synagogue or temple and tries to kill us? What if we decide to go to Israel and there's a bombing or a violent attack? What if we host a joyous life event or cultural gathering and someone tries to disrupt it and/or target us? What if my child wears a Jewish star necklace or a kippah/yarmulke in public and is attacked for being Jewish?*

Our fears are real and understandable. They get to the heart of Jewish anxiety about power—how Jews deploy it as a tiny minority in the world (especially in Israel), and how power might be used against Jews as individuals or as a group, simply because we are Jewish.

However, our habits in response to fear and uncertainty are *choices.* When we're activated into the Four F's and make behavior choices from that constricted location in our brains, we choose control, avoidance, distraction, and over-saturation strategies that often makes our anxiety *worse.* And when we do this to ourselves repeatedly, thinking that these strategies will somehow make us feel better and take the pain away, we suffer terribly.

MAPPING YOUR JEWISH ANXIETY HABITS ABOUT SAFETY

What do you notice about any tension you might be holding in your body right now? I invite you to take a moment to journal some thoughts and breathe deeply. Now, I invite you to turn your attention to mapping your own specific anxiety habits. Remember that anxiety is a combination of fear, plus uncertainty, *plus our habits.*

This is a learning exercise you can do many times, to increase your awareness of your habits and their results. My hope is that as you map your habits, you choose to practice curiosity, kindness and compassion for yourself, rather than judgment, inner criticism, or self-shaming. Notice what happens in your body as you consider these questions and write down any insights you might have in your answers.

- If you grew up Jewish, how did your elders actively transmit stories of Jewish trauma and suffering as Jewish identify-building education? How did that influence your own perceptions and experience of the world as a Jew? What stories of Jewish resilience did you learn, if any?
- If you embraced Judaism as an adult, what have you noticed about how people in your community respond to the world, especially when there's an incident of anti-Jewish oppression? How have these communal responses shaped your own experience of being and feeling Jewish in the world?
- If you have children or grandchildren, how do you tell stories about the Jewish past, present, and future? Do you emphasize Jewish lack of safety? Do you tend to focus on Jewish resilience?

Now let's return to the habit loop of cues, sensations, feelings, thoughts, needs, behaviors, and results that you learned in Chapter 2.

1. Cues. Bring to mind an example of when you felt anxious about something related to feeling Jewishly unsafe. You might want to choose an experience that registers at a 5 out of 10 on the anxiety scale, rather than the most difficult example, which might prompt a freeze response. Take a moment to remember or describe in specific detail where you were, and what was happening at that moment. Who or what might have triggered your fear and uncertainty about feeling unsafe?

2. Sensations. What do you remember happening in your body when you experienced that trigger, if anything? Do you remember any feelings of tightness or contraction? What did you notice about the places in your body where you typically hold tension, such as your brow, jaw, shoulders, neck, or back? Do you remember noticing any changes in your breathing? Knowing what you now know about the Four F's (fight, flight, freeze, fawn), can you identify the kind of stress response your brain deployed in that to help you feel and stay safe?

3. Feelings. What were some feelings you had in response to the cue or trigger of feeling othered? How did you feel about the other person/people, and how did you feel about yourself? If you can easily identify the basic human emotions, can you dig deeper and identify some more complex feelings in response to feeling unsafe?

4. Thoughts. What were your thoughts about the person, people, or situation that felt unsafe or uncertain? What were your thoughts about yourself? Did you immediately move into catastrophizing a worst-case scenario? Did you engage in exit strategy planning (a flight response), or imagine how to fight back in anger?

5. Needs. Understanding our needs can be tricky, especially when we're in our amygdala, not in our pre-frontal cortex. When we feel afraid, uncertain, or threatened, our body responds with survival mode strategies. What do you think you needed in that moment when you felt Jewishly othered? Did you need to feel safer? Did you need reassurance about your physical and/or emotional safety? Did you need to feel seen and validated for who you are, understood, and more connected to whoever you were interacting with? Did you need to feel respected and affirmed for your inherent dignity and worth?

6. Behaviors. What behavior or action did you take in response to feeling afraid or uncertain? What did you choose, whether consciously or not, from one of the Four F's to fight, flee, freeze, or fawn to deal with the experience? Did you choose an action to try to control the situation? Did you try to avoid or distract yourself from the uncomfortable, upsetting, or possibly unsafe situation? Did you over-saturate yourself with vicarious trauma exposure in any way as a control response?

*7. **Results.*** What was the outcome of that experience and the behavioral choices you made in response to your embodied sensations, thoughts, feelings, and needs? Did you feel better, the same, or worse after moving through that habit loop? Did your existing neural pathways of inherited Jewish trauma strengthen that network? Did you increase or decrease your Jewish vicarious trauma? I'm asking these questions with the deepest compassion, not judgment, for you and for all of us. What might be the learning for you individually about this reflective exercise in mapping out a safety habit? What might be the implications for our communities if we looked with compassion at our Jewish anxiety habits in response to safety fears?

After answering these questions, I invite you to pause and simply breathe into your body. Notice with compassion where you might feel tight in your body. Notice your breathing. Maybe pause before reading the next section so that you can metabolize your insights about your safety needs and habits. When you feel calm, centered, and ready, it's time to move on to Jewish shame habits about our worth and dignity.

JEWISH SHAME: INTERNALIZING ANTI-JEWISH CONTEMPT AND DISGUST

I felt not Jewish enough as a kid because my dad wasn't Jewish. I've wondered whether I would be accepted or rejected

In the previous chapter, we explored how anti-Jewish oppression dumps its toxic blame, shame, aggression, othering, and violence on Jews. We've *throughout my life. When I was in grade school, a friend said, "I'm glad you're not Jewish," when we were talking about video games. I was so confused—what did that mean? I didn't say anything, and I told my mom, she was furious. We stopped being friends after that. I'm sure that he heard something in his family that it was ok to be friends because we weren't really Jewish. My mom always said that she felt out of place in the Midwest, because she was from Queens. I remember people making jokes in college that were anti-Jewish, in jest, but weren't funny. I got used to it. I never hid my background, but I never publicly went out and talked about being Jewish.*

—Adam, thirties

As a kid in third grade, there was one other Jew in my class, Michael. I decided to blend in that year, and I didn't want to stand out as a Jew and light the Chanukah candles. Michael said I wasn't a good Jew because I didn't want to light the candles – that was my childhood shame of wanting to blend in. Man, did that hurt and I still remember

explored how that hatred factors into our safety habits. Now I want to look at how this oppression influences our own sense of inherent worth and dignity as human beings, and as Jews. Prentiss Hemphill, in *What It Takes to Heal,* describes worth and dignity as the "capacity to feel inherent value simply in the fact that we exist."[35]

We are worthy of love, care, and respect, no matter what the world tells us, no matter how contemptuously the world treats Jews with disgust and revulsion. This idea of our inherent worthiness, *simply because we exist,* is grounded in Jewish wisdom and it weaves its way throughout the vast library of Jewish sacred text. Indeed, in the very first chapter of Genesis, the author writes, "Let us make humanity in our image, after our likeness.... And the Divine created humanity in the image of the Divine." What does it mean to be created in the likeness and imagine of the Divine?

Rabbi Moshe Chaim Luzzatto, an eighteenth-century Italian Kabbalist, writes that "the physical human form is the embodiment of all the Divine qualities together, and demonstrates everything that can be understood about the Divine presence."[36] Luzzatto riffs on how each human

how much it hurt. I still don't think I'm a good Jew—I don't keep kosher, and I don't really go to synagogue.
—Richard, seventies

being's existence (transcending our Jewish particularity) embodies a Divine spark of mysterious aliveness, just like the mysterious aliveness of Life Unfolding (what some people call God). In other words, we are sacred because we are created from an ultimately mysterious, unknowable source of Sacredness. We matter, we are worthy, simply because we are alive.

This idea of the inherent dignity and sacredness of human beings informs our relationships to Jewish texts, ethics, and one another. My fervent hope is that we can remember our inherent dignity and act from a place of love towards ourselves, especially when we feel scared or unworthy because of anti-Jewish oppression. Remembering our inherent dignity is a better alternative to shaming ourselves that we're unworthy of love and care.

But it's easy to forget or question our worth and dignity when we are consistently, perniciously othered, whether from anti-Jewish contempt, or in combination with other forms of oppression, such as sexism, ableism, racism, and homophobia. When the world does not mirror back our inherent value, when people express contempt, ignorance, indifference, or hostility towards Jews and Judaism, we internalize that oppression as shame. We come to believe that we are unworthy and inadequate. Many of us constantly feel an inchoate, anxious unease and looping self-punishing thoughts, a sense that however we are Jewishly (and other identities), somehow, we're not enough.

This is why people come to my office and begin our conversation with what they're not: I'm not religious, I don't believe in God, I don't keep kosher, I don't go to temple, I don't know Hebrew. I'm a bad Jew because I have a Christmas tree, my partner is not Jewish, I hated Hebrew school, etc. It's pervasive, persistent, and utterly painful to witness.

These examples of shaming ourselves are damaging forms of self-harm, a maladaptive response to the contempt and disgust of feeling othered by the world. Let me be clear: there are absolutely *no positive benefits* to shaming ourselves. Shame does not motivate us to be better human beings. Sadly, many of us harm ourselves with internalized shame, all the time, out of habit. Most Jewish people I know carry deep shame about our worthiness as Jews, but we don't have the language to name it. Internalized Jewish shame influences how we perceive ourselves, especially in our (usually unconscious) unmet, basic human needs for safety, recognition, connection, affirmation and validation that we are worthy of love, respect, and care.

Most typical Jewish shame responses involve flight, freeze or fawn strategies. We avoid taking up space or drawing attention to ourselves as Jews. Some of us overwork and become so busy, status-oriented, and achievement focused, we're like hummingbirds who don't know how to relax. We avoid necessary rest, avoid connecting with our ancestors and our community, and avoid exploring our yearnings for meaning through Jewish learning and wisdom. We engage in if-then thoughts, feelings, and behaviors that gloss over what we really might need by thinking: if I just try harder, work harder, blend in more, make myself smaller, take up less space, smile more, change my appearance, then I will be worthy of care, love, and respect. Some of us try to shed any markers of distinctiveness to pass as white (if possible) and not identify as "too Jewish," so that we won't draw attention to ourselves and become targets. Some of us engage in deeply grooved patterns of people pleasing (fawning) in the hopes that others will like us and not reject, abandon, or hurt us.

Internalized shame influences whether and how we connect with one another as Jews, and whether/how we avoid or flee from Jewish connection. It shapes how we judge and reject other Jews (and people from other spiritual traditions), because their different way of being in the world triggers our fear. Then many of us turn that internalized shame around into projections of disgust and contempt for other Jews.

I see this pattern of expressing disgust toward other Jews as forms of lateral violence and distress intolerance of Jewish differences. For example, many of us (from the political right to the left, from secular and observant) harbor stereotypes and distorted perceptions of other Jews who look, think, and behave differently than we do. The unconscious thought loop goes something like this: *They're not really Jewish, because they don't [you fill in the blank].* Or conversely, *They're too much [Jewish fundamentalists, crazy, etc.] because they look/act/observe Judaism differently than me.* This also comes up frequently with Jewish liturgical music and prayer innovations. Every year, when my rabbinic team gently introduces a new tune to a familiar prayer, such as *Oseh Shalom*, the prayer for peace, invariably someone comes up to me with a judgmental tone in their voice, or writes a nasty comment in our survey, about how that's not the *right way* to sing the prayer. The implicit critique is that there's only one right way, that encountering diverse Jewish approaches threatens one's own fragile and unstable sense of Jewishness.

The results of internalized shame and its counterpart of rejection and judgment are painful. We become estranged from ourselves and other Jews. We engage in internal self-harming monologues. We disengage Jewishly in building community across our Jewish differences. We give away our power to choose how to care for ourselves with compassion and stand up for ourselves in the world as enough. We learn, unconsciously, to think and feel that somehow, *we* are deficient, that *we* are unworthy of respect, care, and love. We learn to assume that there's something wrong with *us*, rather than something being wrong with the way power is distributed, that there's something deeply wrong with our unequal, divided world as it is. This manifests as a looping internal track that we're bad Jews: either too much or not enough. Instead of pausing to discern what we might need when shame arises, we immediately move to criticize ourselves, judge others, and self-flagellate. What would our lives look like if we practiced more self-compassion and kindness, rather than negative shaming habits about who we are as Jews?

TOO MUCH AND NOT ENOUGH

I have a lot of introspective anxiety come up during the Jewish High Holidays. Have I offended someone? Sometimes it leads to obsessive worrying about people being upset with me. I think there's a sense of being exceptional and chosen, which is the flip side of stereotype that we control the world. Then I feel like I'm not enough, I'm not helping, I'm insufficient in what I'm doing in the world.

—Sam, thirties

When Jews are depicted in threatening, grandiose conspiracy fantasies online by white supremacists as all-powerful and controlling, this adds to our existing Jewish shame, particularly around issues of money and power. Whenever anyone Jewish commits some sort of financial crime (for example, Bernie Madoff and more recently, Sam Bankman-Fried), I internally cringe and want to hide, a flight response to my own shame about *other* Jewish people's terrible behavior. Sometimes I have said out loud, "How could they do this? Don't they understand this is bad for the Jews?" I feel ashamed, alarmed, and disappointed that these individuals' criminal behavior will only solidify anti-Jewish perceptions that Jews only care about money. This is a typical "model minority" response, that everyone who is Jewish is overly responsible for representing all Jews, and therefore, we must always be on our best behavior, otherwise we'll let someone, or our entire people down. We live in anxious fear of disappointing others, which came up in most of my interviews, especially with Jewish women. Abby, in her thirties, describes this worry:

> I feel anxious when I worry that I'm going to let someone down. If I feel like someone is going to be disappointed in me, if I don't do something well or deliver on a promise or I'm late. The anxiety of someone else being disappointed in me feels terrible. I will expend a lot of mental energy and worry on trying to disappoint someone. I don't want to BE a disappointment—which is my shame, I AM—my being is a disappointment.

When we're stereotyped in movies, books, and plays as obsessed with appearances, status and materialism, that prompts our feelings of shame. We internalize those stereotypes with embarrassment and discomfort, and many of us get angry and upset about how we're depicted, especially when the creatives responsible for those depictions are Jewish themselves. We laugh uneasily with recognition of the caricatures but then wonder how people who are not Jewish might be influenced by those terrible stereotypes, and how those stereotypes might then affect how we're seen in the world.

These internalized shame habits are more difficult to untangle when we look through the lens of intersectionality—the idea that oppression based on identity is never one-dimensional. For Jews who inhabit additional marginalized identities (people of color, women and non-binary people, differently abled folks, queers, identifiably religious Jews, working class and poor Jews, anti-Zionist Jews), the too much/not enough shaming tropes are complicated. Our bodies and body parts are considered too big, our skin color might be considered too dark, we're too loud, we might walk and talk too fast, we're too direct or we interrupt too much, and/or we're too Jewish in how we practice Judaism.

Conversely, we might feel plagued by those repetitive anxious thoughts that we're somehow not Jewish enough. In my early days of rabbinical school, I used to imagine a male, older, Hasidic rebbe sitting on my shoulder tsk tsking me, that whatever I was doing, it would never be good or authentic enough.

Underneath all the anti-Jewish internalized shaming is a pernicious and destructive idea: who do you think you are? Who do you think you are to take up any space? Who do you think you are to exercise Jewishly creative agency and power? How dare you think that whatever you're doing or thinking or saying, it's enough? How dare you think you're deserving of care, respect, and love? These are painful, habitual thoughts and feelings that harm us.

Do any of these tropes feel or sound familiar in your lived experience? If yes, you are not alone. If you're nodding your head in recognition, now might be a good time to journal some of the not enough/too much habitual thoughts and feelings you carry. Here are some initial questions to consider:

- If you grew up Jewish, what kinds of messages did you inherit, observe, or learn from your family of origin about being inherently worthy of care and love? What did you inherit, observe, or learn about being too Jewish or not Jewish enough? What did you learn from the community and wider culture in which you grew up? How did these messages and experiences dovetail with other identities you might carry in the world where too much/not enough are salient for you? How did what you learned influence your own thoughts, feelings, perceptions and experiences of feeling like you're not okay Jewishly, as well as any other identity you hold?
- If you embraced Judaism as an adult, what have you experienced, observed, or learned regarding messages that you're too much/not enough as a Jew? How do people in your community express these

habits? How have these communal responses shaped your own experience of being and feeling Jewish in the world?

MAPPING JEWISH ANXIETY HABITS ABOUT WORTH, DIGNITY, AND SHAME

I offer this next set of questions with the deepest care and compassion. Mapping our anxiety habits in response to feeling ashamed is one of the hardest and most potentially transformative steps we can take towards becoming kinder and more compassionate toward ourselves. It can also bring up a lot of difficult feelings about how we've unconsciously internalized contempt and disgust and turned that on ourselves in the form of self-shaming and inner criticism.

I suggest mapping only one habit at a time. Then you can put this book down to metabolize whatever feelings and insights came up for you, and practice love, compassion, and kindness towards yourself to re-regulate your nervous system. You can always come back to this section to map different anxiety habits as you deepen your practices of kindness and compassion and discernment that we'll explore in the following chapters. Please be kind to yourself, unlearning our Jewish anxiety habits is a lifelong process of discovery, discernment, and growth.

1. Cues: Can you identify a too much/not enough habit loop that is alive for you? If you have several of these habits, just focus on one that is less triggering, so that you can create some distance from the difficult feelings that might arise. What are the cues or moments where you have felt this not enough/too much habit? What aspect of your Jewishness does it focus on? What is happening and who are you with when this habit loop begins?

2. Sensations: when you experience the feeling of not enough/too much, what happens in your body? Do you feel tight or expansive in your breathing, open or closed in your bodily awareness? Does any specific area in your body feel hot, cold, clenched, or constricted?
3. Thoughts and Feelings: what feelings or thoughts arise when any worth, dignity, or shame habits come up? Do those feelings include any shades of fear, sadness, anger, or disgust? What are some typical thought loops you observe? Do those thoughts make you feel better or worse? Do you hear an inner critical voice, and if so, what does that voice say to you, about yourself? Now that you're noticing the thoughts, what strikes you as true or untrue about them? What might be helpful or unhelpful about those thoughts?
4. Needs: When you're in that habit loop moment about feeling/thinking/being too much or not enough, what do you think are some unmet needs? Do you have a need for recognition, validation, or affirmation of your inherent worth? Do you need reassurance that you're enough as you are? Do you need comforting about something that you didn't get growing up, or solidarity that you're not alone in feeling this way? Do you have a wish or a need for someone to offer repair for any harm that gets triggered when you're in this habit loop?
5. Behaviors: What are the actions or behaviors you typically choose when you're in this habit? Do you move towards connection with others or avoidance or rejection? Do you try to distract yourself from feeling any discomfort? Do you try hard to prove

your worth to yourself or to others for affirmation? Do you engage in self-deprecation or minimization of your inherent worth? Do you engage in contempt or disgust towards yourself or towards other people?

6. Results: What do you get from this habit? Can you identify any positive rewards, or any negative results? What do the results of this habit feel like in your body? Does the habit amplify or increase any tightness or tension in your body, or does it result in feelings of relaxation, expansion, or openness? If you close your eyes, put a hand on your heart right now, and take a few deep breaths, what do you notice? Does anything in your body change as you notice your breath? As you breathe, take a moment to practice gratitude for how your body responds to the breath as a lifegiving force. This is a gift you can give to yourself as part of your unlearning process. Remember, you are worthy of love, respect, and care, simply because you are alive. You don't have to earn or prove anything.

BELONGING AND ACCEPTANCE

At school, where I work, there aren't many of us who are Jewish. I have to explain every single thing, because they just don't know. They had a secret Santa, and I didn't want to do it, and I said so, and they were like "So?" They didn't get it—it's a Christian holiday, no matter how secular it gets. And then

I want to share a vulnerable story about the yearning to belong. When I was in graduate school in the '90s, I spent a lot of time trying to decode the secret, magical formula for how to write in academese. I felt like I was expected to think, speak, and write in a confusing new language with opaque conceptual jargon, if I wanted to participate in conversations with

I was tokenized after that, if anything Jewish came up, they would ask me "Is this ok?" The energy is always weird for people who don't really know anything and they're afraid they're going to say something wrong. There are some spaces where I'm fine with educating, and other spaces where I don't want to do it.

—Simon, thirties

One of the major ways my anxiety shows up is being overly concerned with what people think of me. It affects my day-to-day life because I edit myself a lot. I have a lot of thoughts and opinions and insights, and often I don't share because I'm nervous. I could offend someone; I could make myself appear like I'm not a good person. I would like to be able to share my voice without inhibition from anxiety. I think it interferes with my ability to connect with people sometimes and that's a loss. It usurps my whole experience.

—Shaina, forties

I had a neighbor next door, one day we were playing basketball, and he said to me that he was going to hell if he played

fellow students and teachers. I became an expert in the pretentious academic art of the colon in titles: saying two clever, obtuse things when you could just say one.

After a few years, I began to think, speak and write academese all the time, internally with myself, with friends, and my family. (Thank you to my family for putting up with my pretentiousness, I know it was insufferable.) I would agonize writing sentences and paragraphs with a running internal, highly critical monologue. Was this paragraph referencing enough research to demonstrate my familiarity and competency in the relevant academic literature? Did I make a compelling argument that moved seamlessly from point to point? Did I provide enough qualitative data to prove my theoretical arguments? Did I sound academic enough to get published? I so desperately wanted to belong as a scholar that I contorted myself and lost my authentic voice.

I also wanted to study American Jewish culture. My two graduate school advisors were secular, leftist Jews born in the early 1940s. When I sought their counsel about my dissertation topic, to study gender inequality and American immigration to *basketball with kids who weren't Mormon. That really upset me. I was very guarded after that; it affected me very strongly. We're taught to be humble and to walk softly. I think some of that is keeping your head down and trying not to attract attention as a Jew. I'm always the one who is trying to blend in.*

—Richard, seventies

Israel, they admonished me to reconsider. They worried I wouldn't get an academic job by studying Jews. They didn't think Jews "counted" as part of the sociological conversation about racism, ethnicity, oppression, and inequality. After all, in their minds, Jews were white and they had "made it"—what was there to study? These were painful conversations, and I felt angry, hurt, and confused. Not all Jews were white, and I knew studying Jews was interesting and worthy enough. I had no words for it at the time, but I sensed that their resistance to studying Jews had to do with their own struggles to make it as Jews in academia. I decided not to take their advice. But it took me another twenty-five years to unlearn academese and rediscover my authentic voice through writing this book.

One of our deepest yearnings as human beings is to be accepted and to belong to a larger group. We want to belong to something beyond just our individual selves. For Jews, peoplehood and belonging are the core of Judaism, as a source of strength, comfort and refuge. Throughout the Torah, the Divine gives instructions to Moses for the Israelites, describing this ragtag group of formerly enslaved people repeatedly as a sacred community. It takes a group of ten to form a *minyan* (a Jewish prayer group). In *Pirkei Avot* (Ethics of Our Ancestors, chapter 2:4), Rabbi Hillel says "do not separate yourself from the community."[37] We can create that sense of belonging and connection enlisting Jewish sacred texts, spiritual practices, rituals. These are also the keys to unlocking our freedom from anxiety habits.

But feeling a sense of belonging can be difficult in a culture dominated by Christianity, assimilation pressures, white supremacy, and individualism. For centuries, Jewish acceptance and belonging have been contingent on conforming to standards and norms we didn't create, where the pressure to assimilate raised the stakes for belonging. For example, in my interviews, almost everyone mentioned a constant sense of feeling excluded right after Halloween, when the Christmas marketing season kicks off. Leora, in her sixties, and Rebecca, in her forties, share:

> Christmas for me is a huge trigger. It's two months of incessant Christmas cheer that has absolutely nothing to do with me. It's extremely alienating, and it hasn't gotten any better. We get Sirius XM radio. They have a Chanukah channel that runs from December 23 for a week, and it doesn't follow the Jewish calendar. Does the lack of intent (of being othered) make it ok? Does misgendering a trans person make it ok? Ignorance is really frustrating, especially in stores that want to sell us stuff. Could you just get it right?
>
> There are so many people who were raised with benign Christian traditions or just Christmas. The symbolism for them is that trees and Santa are not religious at all. They're commercial and secular culture—this is American. Trying to explain to them what it feels like as a Jew to experience those things is really hard. It's hard for them to understand. They don't get it at all, they've never had to think about this. For me, there's an added layer—why do I have such an aversion to Christmas trees in public settings? It bothers me SO MUCH, and now I'm really thinking about it and trying to explain it. It produces some anxiety about having to prove

> yourself—what I think, and feel is real, it's not just me being too sensitive.

It is understandable that we might feel anxious if we routinely experience othering, contempt, invisibility or its inverse, hypervisibility as token Jews asked or expected to represent *all* Jews. It's also difficult to feel a sense of belonging when people from the dominant culture express obliviousness or disinterest in actually learning about our people and our culture. The truth is that the juggernaut of Christmas capitalism is not going to change any time soon. How can we care for our nervous systems during this time of year, so that we suffer less from a constant sense of exclusion? What alternative choices are available to us that honor who we are as Jews and our need to belong?

If doubting our worth is the *internalization* of anti-Jewish contempt, changing who we are is an *external* response to our need to belong. Sometimes, without realizing it, we shrink, contort, or hide to blend in. We keep our heads down, and suppress big feelings, in service of acceptance. My grandmother Bessie always said, with a hint of resignation and bitterness in her voice, "Don't rock the boat." I now understand the painful losses that come with that strategy.

For those of us with multiple identities where we navigate oppression, we learn early on to code switch and conform, to be seen as good enough to belong. And painfully, we sometimes learn to adapt and shrink ourselves in response to fellow Jews who unconsciously exclude and other us, with judgmental comments and inappropriate questions that betray their own misperceptions that we don't fully belong in Jewish spaces. Some of us expend lots of energy worrying about being exemplary and perfect, lest we be singled out, shamed, or rejected by others. This is all about squeezing ourselves because of the unequal distribution of power. Petra (she/they), who identifies as queer and, in their forties, describes this phenomenon vividly:

> As far as anxiety goes, it has always been around wanting to be good, do good, and to be a good girl. For me, it's less around success and achievement and more around not wanting to screw up and make mistakes. It's always about when I think I've made a mistake, stepped out of line, or angered an authority figure. I always worry that I've screwed up or someone is hurting because of something I did. I did some work with a therapist who had an interesting perspective on generational trauma. What came up was that some of this anxiety I deal with are echoes of generational trauma, specifically religious trauma, around being good, behaving, keeping your head down, because to step out of line is to be noticed in a way that's extremely dangerous.

This was my undocumented immigrant grandfather's strategy of changing his name from Yossl Leibl Itzkowitz, of Mlawa, Poland to Jorge Itzkowitz in Mexico City, to George Louis in Chicago, and his unsuccessful attempt to shed his Yiddish inflected, Mexican Spanish accented English. This was why my maternal grandmother Naomi dyed her hair bright red, contemptuously eschewed anything Jewish, and restricted her food intake to be considered attractive—"for a Jew." This is why I grew up watching other Jewish girls starve themselves, alter their noses through rhinoplasty, and straighten their textured hair to be accepted as popular. So many of our Jewish anxiety habits are unconscious, assimilationist forms of fawning: people pleasing in the hopes that we will be found worthy of love and acceptance, that we will find acceptance.

Our anxiety habits in response to the desire to belong manifest in magical thinking (if/then), perfectionism and control. We deeply internalize our country's Protestant ethic and economic system: we are only valuable and accepted if we are considered productive workers. If we work as hard as we can, then we'll be indispensable to others, and we'll be accepted. If we constantly strive to achieve, then we'll be accepted as acceptable. If we adapt to dominant norms, then we'll be liked and not excluded or harmed. If we overwork, overdo, and overcompensate, then we'll feel included. No matter that it might come with a serious cost. Sam, in his thirties, describes this pattern:

> I sometimes feel like I have to be good in public—representing the Jews, especially about money, I don't want to be perceived as stingy. I feel obligated to give tzedakah [charity or a righteous action] to homeless people on the street. I don't want someone thinking I'm a stingy Jew. For example, at an event last night, I stayed at the event later than I wanted, because I felt like I had to keep going, even though I was hungry. I felt like I had to do more than anyone else because I want Jews to be seen as doing the good thing.

It makes sense that we want to be seen as good people. Who doesn't? Sam mentions the obligation to give *tzedakah,* to engage in acts of repairing the world, known as *tikkun olam* in Hebrew. So many of us have been inculcated with this wonderful imperative, articulated in Deuteronomy 16: "Justice, justice shall you pursue, that you may thrive and live in the land that the Divine is giving you." We learn that it's part of the Jewish mission to engage in *tikkun olam*—to make the world a better place, to fix the brokenness, to act in service of healing. But this imperative becomes more complicated when we feel like we urgently need to do something and represent all Jews, all the time, because we worry about anti-Jewish stereotypes and contempt. Adina, in her seventies, speaks directly to this association between wanting to do something, and giving *tzedakah* as a response to anxiety:

> When I'm worried about something, I start to say, "What can I do so that I feel more in control?" and then I let go of what I can't control. I plan for situations that might arise so that I'm not blindsided by them. It makes me feel more in control. I donate to causes that are important to me like Hillel on campus and Magen David Adom. When I participate in tikkun olam, I feel better.

I want to be clear here: I cherish the Jewish values of justice and repair. And yet I wonder if our Jewish practice of urgently feeling the need to fix all the time inadvertently contributes to our anxiety. What do we get from these habits? I have seen so many Jewish friends, colleagues, and community members struggle with these anxiety habits that lead to exhaustion, burnout, and discomfort with caring for ourselves.

I write about this from difficult personal experience. Before I began this work of unlearning my own Jewish anxiety, I overworked incessantly. I always felt a sense of urgency and the need to control. I wanted to fit in, and I wanted to be the best at everything I did, out of a nagging perfectionism that I wouldn't be accepted if I didn't run myself into the ground. I felt consumed by an overwhelming need to fix what was broken in the world, and this fueled my social justice organizing. I avoided taking time off, and unconsciously I equated rest with laziness. Who was I if I wasn't always productive, striving, and achieving? This anxiety habit, rooted in unconscious beliefs about my internal worth, and a yearning to be accepted, reached its apex ten years ago, when I was working full-time, attending rabbinical school, and volunteering on my seminary's student board. With that pace, everything in my life suffered—my parenting, my relationships, and my work. Not surprisingly, I burned out and almost dropped out of rabbinical school halfway through.

Here are some questions to consider as you look at any anxiety habits related to the yearning for belonging and acceptance.

- What kinds of messages did you inherit, observe, or learn from your family of origin about belonging? What did you feel like you needed to do or be to feel accepted by friends and family? What did you learn from the wider culture about hiding, shrinking, passing, fawning, or squeezing yourself into something to be considered acceptable? What did you learn about perfectionism or magical if/then thinking? Are there ways you've responded to these messages with habits that come with any costs? How did these messages and experiences dovetail with other identities you might carry in the world?
- If you embraced Judaism as an adult, what have you experienced, observed, or learned about belonging and acceptance as a Jew? What messages have you received and internalized about Jewish belonging and acceptance? How have you had to adapt who you are to fit into your Jewish community? How do people in your community express or project their own anxieties or worry about belonging onto you? How have these communal responses shaped your own experience of being and feeling Jewishly accepted in the world?

Take a few moments to journal some thoughts, feelings, and observations in response to these questions. Then you can pause, breathe, and put this away for a while. When you feel ready to start mapping some habits, pick just one to start slow, because these habits go to the heart of what we yearn for, and unlearning them is a lifelong practice.

MAPPING OUR JEWISH ANXIETY HABITS OF BELONGING AND ACCEPTANCE

As you move through the anxiety loop circle questions below, I invite you to explore your responses with kindness, compassion, and curiosity. What insights arise from the process of mapping your habits around yearning to belong and be accepted? What do you notice in your body as you move through the questions? When you are finished mapping a habit, please put the book down and engage in some lovingkindness and self-care. Mapping our habits can sometimes bring up big feelings that we need to metabolize in the body. You can always come back to these questions to map additional habits you might want to work on.

1. Cues: what are some triggers that set off a belonging habit? Are there any moments on the yearly calendar, such as Christmas or Easter? Are there any moments of recognition you had in reading other people's patterns and experiences from this chapter?
2. Sensations: when you are in this particular habit, what happens in your body? What are some of the sensations you experience? What do you notice about your breathing? Are there places in your body where you hold tension or contraction when you're feeling anxious about belonging or being accepted? Are there ways that you ignore what's happening in your body and just plow onwards?
3. Feelings: Do you notice any feelings around loss of control or fears of rejection? When you're feeling anxious, do you feel an urgent need to *do something*

to address the discomfort, or engage in some sort of fixing? Do you avoid negative feelings of potential rejection or exclusion by overcompensating?

4. Thoughts: what are some of the thoughts that typically come up when you're feeling anxious about belonging or being accepted? Do you worry about someone criticizing or getting mad at you? Do you "should" all over yourself about your human imperfections and limitations? Do you have thoughts about needing to represent all Jews to prevent people from thinking poorly about Jews? Do you engage in magical if/then thinking?
5. Needs: when you're feeling worried, scared, or uncertain about being accepted, what do you *really* need in those moments? Do you need to feel seen as a Jew (and any other identity you might hold)? Do you need to receive love and care, rather than judgment or (worse) indifference? Do you need reassurance that you're OK the way you are? Do you need validation and affirmation about your inherent worth? Do you need to pause, rest and reset, rather than busy yourself and overwork?
6. Behaviors: What are the behaviors and actions you typically chose in response to all these challenging thoughts, feelings, and needs? How might those behaviors be rooted in flight or fawn responses to stress?
7. Results: What happens in your body during this particular habit loop? Do you find yourself energized or rested? Do you get fatigued or resentful? Does your habit alleviate whatever thoughts and feelings arise, or does your typical response amplify those uncomfortable feelings and thoughts?

When you've mapped out some patterns and insights in answering these questions, take a moment to pause. Take a few deep breaths. Notice any tension in your body and breathe fresh oxygen into those tight places. Notice with kindness what's happening in your mind. You're on the cusp of deeper understanding of your habits. This is a moment of potential transformation. We can all adopt a growth mindset of kindness, compassion, curiosity, and courage to find different and better alternatives to any anxiety habits that cause you suffering. That's where we're heading next.

Chapter 5

PAUSE, BREATHE, LISTEN WITH *KINDFULNESS*

> "And Jacob's humility stirred Esau's compassion, so that Esau ran to meet him and embraced him and fell on his neck and kissed him; and they both wept."
>
> **—Genesis 33:4**

How do we unlearn our Jewish anxiety habits? Is it even possible? I think the answer is an unequivocal yes. So far, we've learned how to map some of our habits that amplify Jewish anxiety. With this growing awareness, we can deploy resources from our inherited ancestral wisdom, instead of reacting from trauma or shame.

In this chapter, you'll learn some better alternatives with Jewish values, texts, and practices. The three steps I'll explore here are simple, yet profound: pause, breathe, and listen with *kindfulness,* rather than judgment or harshness. But before we dive in, I want to share a few thoughts about how to engage with Jewish texts, and about the concept of *mitzvot:* action that shows care, which are key to understanding our alternatives to our anxiety habits.

FEELING ANXIOUS ABOUT LEARNING JEWISH TEXTS AND PRACTICES?

Maybe you have considerable experience with Jewish text study and spiritual practice. Maybe you feel like an absolute beginner. I have some good news: it doesn't matter where you are on your learning journey. Jewish wisdom is available to *anyone* with curiosity and an openness to learning. Similarly, Jews hold diverse assumptions and ideas about the origin and authorship of Jewish texts. Some Jews view these texts, like the Torah (or Hebrew Bible) as written by human beings over centuries (often called source criticism or the documentary hypothesis). Some Jews believe these words were written by a Divine source.

I view Jewish texts through the kabbalistic metaphors of a flowing river and a flowering garden: these are ancient, evolving, unfolding, ongoing, and culturally specific discussions across time, space, and generations, about the meaning and purpose of life. Jewish texts offer us the opportunity, in conversation with our ancestors, to apply Jewish wisdom and create meaning in our own lives today. In *Pirkei Avot* 6:1 (Ethics of Our Ancestors) Rabbi Meir teaches, "Anyone who engages in Torah for its own sake merits many things and moreover, makes the entire world worthwhile." The idea of Torah referenced here is called *Torah lishma,* learning for learning's sake, in service of creating meaning in our lives, with a spirit of openness, wonder, and curiosity.

The Jewish texts and practices I offer here provide different road maps for how we might live more purpose, joy, compassion, justice, and connection. It's not about believing the texts are truth with a capital T. Jewish text study as a spiritual practice invites us to ask how a text or a practice might resonate with your own lived experience and insights. It's about engaging Jewish wisdom to discern and deploy potentially different habits with better results than worry, anxiety, and fear. We can also engage in that process by understanding how *mitzvot* (actions) help us get there.

MITZVOT: CARE + ACTIONS + REPETITION = HABITS

Jewish wisdom can inform our behavioral choices, called *mitzvot* in Hebrew. *Mitzvot* are the tangible, specific ways we uphold and strengthen sacred relationships in our lives, through our behavior. *Mitzvot* are actions that show care and a connection to what we hold sacred. A classic translation of mitzvot is commandments or obligations, the things we do because we received teachings about these obligations from an authoritative, commanding God. Rabbi Eugene Borowitz, a twentieth-century liberal theologian, rightly pointed out the challenges of the idea of a commanding God, and especially with the metaphor of God as a masculine king.[38] This anthropomorphic and vertical metaphor of power alienates many liberal and secular Jews. In the decades after the traumatic horror of the Holocaust became clearer, Rabbi Borowitz developed the radical concept of covenantal theology—the idea that we are in a sacred relationship with the vast mystery of the universe, and our *mitzvot* can express how we can strengthen and deepen that relationship to awe, wonder, and mystery. And as Rabbi Toba Spitzer shows in her recent book *God Is Here: Reimagining the Divine,* we don't have to rely on alienating, patriarchal tropes. Thankfully, there are so many wonderful, imaginative, evocative metaphors of the Divine in Jewish sacred literature, some of which I will explore in this chapter.[39]

Whether you have a relationship with (pick your Jewish metaphor: voice, water, tree of life, river, garden, source, mystery, oneness, Presence) or not, *mitzvot* are a practical way to consider the actions and behaviors we engage in habitually throughout our day to demonstrate care for ourselves and others. *Mitzvot* reflect our values, and how we uphold what's most sacred, special, or important to use. *Mitzvot* become meaningful habits over time through their repetition, grounding us in spiritual practices and Jewish time. As you move through this chapter, having already mapped out some of your own Jewish anxiety habits, you can ask yourself some questions:

- What are the results and consequences of my *mitzvot* (repetitive actions and habits?)
- Do my *mitzvot* show care, for myself and others?
- Do my actions and habits create suffering?
- If my actions and habits cause suffering, what are some alternative *mitzvot*?

Choosing away from *mitzvot*/actions that generate anxiety is one powerful reward of unlearning our Jewish anxiety habits. Choosing a positive *mitzvah* toward calming yourself when you're worried, spinning out, or ruminating is an even better reward. Our *mitzvot* can help us tap into remembering that we belong to something bigger and that we're inherently worthy. No earning or proving our worth required. As we continue to practice alternative *mitzvot* through repetition, we don't have to spend too much time or energy on deploying them. They just become our go-to resources that inform our habits of being and doing.

WHAT KINDFULNESS IS

> "Awareness affords us choice; it frees us to discern what is wise and useful in this moment. Paying attention to our emotional states frees us to act with wisdom for our sake and the benefit of others."
>
> **—Rabbi Jordan Bendat-Appell,**
> *The Gift of Awareness*[40]

This word I'm using may be unfamiliar to you. It is a portmanteau of kindness, mindfulness, and awareness. Most people have heard of mindfulness, but not *kindfulness*, which was first coined in 2016 by Ajahn Brahm, a British theoretical physicist turned Buddhist monk and dharma teacher.[41]

Mindfulness is more widely known as a secular meditation practice, accessible to anyone, regardless of spiritual or religious background. Jon Kabat-Zinn, the founder of Mindfulness-Based Stress Reduction and a secular Jew, defines mindfulness as "awareness that arises through paying attention, on purpose, in the present moment, non-judgmentally." In research studies over the past several decades, mindfulness practice has been shown to reduce stress, anxiety, and depression.[42] This practice has helped thousands of people live with more equanimity and acceptance of what is arising in the present moment.

Mindfulness encourages the cultivation of our awareness through the simple (but sometimes challenging) practice of seeing our breath and observing our thoughts, feelings, and sensations. This non-theistic approach resonates with many Jews who identify as spiritual, but not religious, and suffer from what I call *post-traumatic God disorder:* an understandable discomfort or antipathy towards gendered and hierarchical metaphors of God as King or Lord. As I explored in earlier chapters, so many Jews lead with the headline, "I'm a bad Jew because I don't believe in God," without realizing that defining oneself by belief, and shaming oneself for theological skepticism of those metaphors, reveals the influence of living in an assimilationist, Christian-dominant society. It's also not an accident that many early contemporary mindfulness teachers are Jewish Baby Boomers. Several important Jewish Buddhist teachers grew up secular and/or alienated from mid-century American Judaism, discovered Vipassana meditation, and brought the practice back to the United States.

But there's more than mindfulness for us.

KINDFULNESS IS A JEWISH VALUE

> "Shimon the Righteous was one of the last of the men of the great assembly. He used to say: the world stands upon three things: Torah (learning), acts of service, and the practice of reciprocal kindness."
>
> **—*Pirkei Avot* 1:2 (Ethics of our Ancestors)**

Chesed is the Hebrew word for kindness or mercy. Kindness is considered a foundational Divine attribute, a quality for us as human beings to emulate. Jewish texts recognize, from the very first chapters of the Torah, that we humans are embedded in a larger web of relational reciprocity, created *b'tzelem Elohim,* in the image and likeness of a Divine Source, and bound together by our actions (mitzvot) that show care and kindness toward one another.

In Jewish tradition, we're invited to see ourselves as having agency and inherent capacity for doing good in the world, and for taking responsibility when we make mistakes and/or cause harm (this concept is called *teshuvah*—returning to our inherent integrity). I'd like to offer some context from the Torah here to explain where, how, and why this Jewish value applies to mindful, non-judgmental awareness of the present moment.

In Exodus chapter 19, the Israelites have left oppression and enslavement in Egypt. They've crossed the Red Sea and have begun a long journey through the desert towards their promised land, Israel. Moses climbs Mount Sinai to receive important instructions for how the Israelites can live together in freedom. These are called the *Aseret HaDibrot,* or the Ten Sayings (you might have learned the phrase "Ten Commandments"). These teachings are the original *mitzvot* in Torah.

Unfortunately, in Moses' absence while up on the mountain, the Israelites become fearful he will never return- an early example of Jewish anxiety! To assuage their fears and insecurities, they build a golden calf to worship. When Moses finally descends from the mountain top, he sees the idol, becomes furious, and (reacting from his amygdala) smashes the 10 Teachings in anger and frustration. It's an understandable, but not necessarily an emotionally well-regulated response to his strong feelings.

Fast forward to Exodus chapter 34. Moses ascends the mountain alone a second time, and he directly asks to see the face of the Divine. The Divine demurs, saying that the experience of face-to-face encounter would be too powerful for Moses to comprehend. Instead, the Divine, in the form of a cloud, passes before Moses and says something extraordinary, in third person, about Divine presence and kindness. This Exodus text is called the thirteen Attributes *(middot* in Hebrew) of the Divine:

וַיַּעֲבֹ֨ר יְהוָ֥ה ׀ עַל־פָּנָיו֮ וַיִּקְרָא֒ יְהוָ֣ה ׀ יְהוָ֔ה אֵ֥ל רַח֖וּם וְחַנּ֑וּן אֶ֥רֶךְ
אַפַּ֖יִם וְרַב־חֶ֥סֶד וֶאֱמֶֽת׃

Va'ya'avor YHVH al panav va'yikra YHVH YHVH el rachum v'chanun, erech apayim v'rav chesed v'emet.

> And the mysterious Source passed by Moses's face and said, "The Source! The Source! A Source compassionate and gracious, slow to anger [literally, long in nostril breathing], overflowing in kindness and truth."

It is important to recognize that compassion and grace are the first attributes in this list, and kindness and truth are the last. All these attributes are variations of what love looks like in action. When we practice compassion toward ourselves and others, that's love in action (there's more on this in a minute). When we offer someone grace after they've made a mistake or hurt us, and dedicate themselves to changing their behavior, that's love in action. When we practice kindness and truth-telling toward ourselves and others, that's love in action.

I don't think it's an accident that the first and last attributes are compassion, kindness, and truth. Indeed, they are connected and interdependent. The Hebrew root of compassion is r-ch-m, which means womb, from where we all emerge into the world. The Ba'al Shem Tov, an eighteenth-century Ukrainian rabbi, considered the founder of Hasidism, wrote, "There is one singular love in the world, and it is the greatest of God's gifts: the *ability* to be compassionate."[43] And in an extraordinary text from the Babylonian Talmud, Berachot 7a, the ancient rabbis imagined how the Divine prays, and what the Divine might pray for, which is compassion:

> Said Rabbi Zutra ben Tuvia in the name of Rav [all different generations of Jewish teachers]: May it be My will that my compassion will conquer my anger, that my compassion will prevail over my other attributes, that I behave towards my children according to the quality of compassion.

The ancient rabbis imagined that even the Source of Mystery was engaged in an ongoing reflective spiritual practice to become kinder and less reactive. They envisioned a Divine Source praying for more compassion!

Kindness, compassion, and truth-telling are ancient Jewish values and practices that can change our lives. Whether you connect to Jewish theology or not, this text invites us to use our imagination and creativity and offers a source text about the Jewish value of kindness and present moment awareness, in service of seeking and finding truth. Here are four questions to consider:

- When have you felt a sense of loving presence, filled with compassion and kindness?

- How does it feel to receive compassion, grace, and kindness from people who care about you?
- What does it feel like to offer compassion, grace, and kindness to others?
- Are there moments in your daily life where you might turn toward yourself with kindness and compassion, rather than harshness or judgment?

There are other ways to understand kindness and compassion. In Latin, the word compassion takes on a different meaning: "to suffer with." With this definition, compassion usually refers to how we show up for others who are suffering. Dr. Kristin Neff, a psychologist at the University of Texas at Austin, has spent the past few decades developing the concept of *self*-compassion, of turning our compassion focus toward being with ourselves and our full humanity when we recognize we're suffering. In *The Science of Mindfulness and Self-Compassion,* with Dr. Shauna Shapiro, she describes self-compassion as the practice of noticing when we're suffering, and turning toward ourselves with warmth and caring, rather than merciless, harsh judgment and criticism. We can recognize that everyone suffers, and we can take comfort in recognizing our own humanity when we're suffering.

> Instead of just ignoring your pain with a "stiff upper lip" mentality, you stop to tell yourself "This is difficult right now, how can I comfort and care for myself in this moment?" Having compassion for yourself means that you honor and accept your humanness. You will encounter frustrations, losses will occur, you will make mistakes, bump up against your limitations, fall short of your ideals. This is the human condition, a reality shared by all of us. The more you open your heart to this reality instead of

> constantly fighting against it, the more you will be able to feel compassion for yourself and all your fellow humans in the experience of life.[44]

It is hard enough to live in a contemptuous, oppressive world, where navigating fear and uncertainty often leaves us feeling stiff-necked, tight, and constricted. It's hard enough to soften the harsh effects of inherited trauma, vicarious trauma, and internalized shame.

Chesed, kindness, and *rachamim,* compassion, are antidotes to Jewish self-shaming. They are Jewish ways to seeing and caring for ourselves more truthfully. Kindness and compassion toward ourselves can soften the blunt, harmful effects of anti-Jewish contempt. It simply feels better to be kind and compassionate toward ourselves than to practice disgust, revulsion, or contempt. It feels better to practice kindness when we're feeling ashamed, afraid, fearful of rejection, or uncertain about our own worth, the way we would easily show up with kindness toward a friend expressing those difficult feelings. We can learn how to practice kindfulness and compassion the moment we realize we're suffering from anxiety, worry, fear, or shame, or when we're projecting those difficult feelings onto others. Let's take a moment now to practice by focusing on just two aspects of our aliveness: our breath that infuses our awareness, and our feet that ground and support us in space.

KINDFULNESS PRACTICE

I encourage you to find a quiet place to sit comfortably, without distractions, for about five minutes. You might want to set your phone timer and then turn off any other sounds to avoid interruptions and close the door where you'll practice, so that you don't feel self-conscious. You can sit in a chair, on the floor, or wherever supports your body in this moment. Gently close your eyes and take a few normal breaths through your nose. Notice your breath as you breathe, how your belly expands and your chest rises on the inhale, and how your body changes and shifts, as you release on exhale. At this point, you might become aware that your thoughts have wandered somewhere other than observing the breath. This is great! I encourage you to kindly, with compassion, bring your attention and awareness back to your breath.

Now, with kindful awareness, notice your feet, which help us feel grounded. Notice whether your toes are clenched or relaxed, whether they're planted on the ground or tucked underneath you. Try to bring your awareness to each individual toe as you inhale and exhale. Feel free to wiggle each toe and notice the sensations that arise in your feet when you wiggle. Do you notice anything different when you bring your awareness to each foot and each toe? If your attention has wandered, bring your awareness back to your breath with kindness and compassion. It's perfectly normal and it's simply what our minds do. Now, bring your awareness to the arches of your feet and your heels and ankles. What do you notice about each of these different parts of your feet that offer you grounding? You can offer warmth, caring, kindness and compassion to your feet for the support they offer your body. Continue to breathe.

Take another few moments to notice with kindness and compassion any sensations, thoughts, and feelings arising from moment to moment. Notice where you're holding tension or clenching your muscles. When you notice any tension, you can simply and kindfully breathe deeply into those tight places and exhale out the constriction with compassion. If you become aware that you've gotten distracted, or that you're having judging or harsh thoughts, or feelings of shame ("I'm a bad meditator, when will this be over?"), simply notice the judgment with compassion and kindness. How might you honor and accept your breath and body with kindness and compassion, rather than harshness or criticism? How might you offer yourself warmth and caring, and perhaps amazement for how your breath and your feet support all the things your body does to function each day?

When the five minutes are up, before gently fluttering your eyes open, you can offer yourself one last kindfulness practice. I often put a hand gently on my heart, bow my head in gratitude for my body and say: "May I be kind to myself and to others. May I be compassionate to myself and to others."

When you finish a kindfulness practice and open your eyes, you can take a moment to notice with curiosity. How do you feel in your body after five minutes of practicing kindfulness and compassion toward yourself? What did you notice or learn about yourself in this experience? Did you feel any different in your body or your mind at the end of your practice than when you began? How might this practice be a better alternative to any Jewish anxiety habits you've identified that you'd like to let go of? You can repeat this practice with your breath and any other body part as many times a day as you'd like.

KINDFULNESS AND HABIT LOOPS

Rabbi Jeff Roth, a wonderful Jewish meditation teacher, writes, "The present moment is the only moment where existence can be directly experienced. The past and future do not exist except as concepts. As awareness expands, we become less identified with our conditioning and freer to respond creatively. Your own life is the perfect vehicle for this practice."[45]

Now that you have one example of a kindfulness practice in your back pocket, let's return to the habit loop in chapter one and think about *mitzvot*—actions that can demonstrate care, kindness, and compassion, as alternatives to judgment, self-criticism, and harshness.

The next time you notice you're feeling a little anxious, that's a perfect opportunity to practice kindfulness and compassion before acting from habit. You can observe the sensations, thoughts, and feelings happening in your body. What just happened to trigger your awareness that you're feeling anxious? How can you simply notice, as a compassionate witness, the thoughts and feelings that are arising? What are the sensations in your body when you notice this? What's happening with your breathing? Do you notice any areas of tightness or clenching in your body?

You can also practice kindfulness and compassion about what you might be needing in that moment. Remember the list of needs identified by Marshall Rosenberg about habit loops? As a refresher, Rosenberg suggested that we all have basic and universal needs, and that our feelings arise from these needs either being met or unmet. These universal needs include sustenance, safety, love, understanding, empathy, creativity, worth (value, recognition, affirmation, and respect), a sense of belonging, autonomy (choice and control over our lives) and meaning. Our needs also include beauty and joy, play and rest, wholeness and harmony, trust and mutuality, fulfillment and well-being. When you realize you're anxious, you can ask yourself, *What is it that I need right now?*

Maybe, in that moment of practicing kindfulness, you realize you need some reassurance about your safety (whether physical or emotional). Maybe you need affirmation that you are worthy of care and respect if someone has just unintentionally or unconsciously engaged in a frustrating microaggression. And finally, consider alternative actions available to you in that moment. What action or behavior do you typically move towards? Is that urge towards a typical action or behavior something that meets your identified need? Or is it something that results in distraction, avoidance or amplification of any discomfort? Most importantly, how might you simply be kind and compassionate to yourself in that moment, and do nothing but notice? What's a better alternative than what you usually reach towards?

SHABBAT FOR YOUR NERVOUS SYSTEM

Two additional unlearning practices are to PAUSE and BREATHE when we feel anxious. Pausing slows down our habit loops to discern what we need in the moment and gives us time to choose different alternatives than our usual anxiety habits of amplification, distraction, or avoidance. Conscious breathing turns our attention back to our bodies, calms us, and resets our nervous system when we feel stressed, scared, and/or not enough. Pause and breathe are better alternatives to Jewish anxiety than responding from the Four F's. Like the practice of kindfulness and self-compassion, the purpose of pause and breathe is to simply be with whatever feelings are arising and allow them to pass. Rather than rush into doing, we can pause and breathe, with kindful awareness and compassion toward ourselves, just as we would toward a friend in distress.

In Hebrew, the word for pause is *hafsakah,* and it literally means to take a break, or to cease from doing. The word for breath in Hebrew is *neshimah*, connected to the word *neshama*: one of two important words for soul. The second important word for embodied soul is *nefesh*, which is also mentioned in Genesis 2. *Neshimah*—our breath literally infuses our soul (*nefesh* and *neshama)* with consciousness, breathing and aliveness. Let's explore this idea with a few Jewish texts about Shabbat, the Jewish day of rest.

Shabbat offers a weekly timeout to *pause and breathe*, and to rest our frazzled nervous systems. Pausing, resting, and ceasing are embedded in the word, meaning, and practice of *Shabbat.* The first mention of Shabbat occurs in the second chapter of Genesis. In the text, the Divine has spent a very busy six days of creating, and then ceases all creation to rest:

וַיְבָ֤רֶךְ אֱלֹהִים֙ אֶת־י֣וֹם הַשְּׁבִיעִ֔י וַיְקַדֵּ֖שׁ אֹת֑וֹ כִּ֣י ב֤וֹ שָׁבַת֙ מִכָּל־
מְלַאכְתּ֔וֹ אֲשֶׁר־בָּרָ֥א אֱלֹהִ֖ים לַעֲשֽׂוֹת׃
Va'yivarech Elohim et yom ha-Shabbat hash'vi'i

va'yikadesh oto ki vo shavat mi'kol melachto asher barah Elohim la'asot.

> And the Source blessed the seventh day and declared it sacred—having stopped on that day all the work of creation that the Source had done.

Four sentences later, we learn of another, very different creation story, about how breath (*neshimah*) infuses our aliveness and our soul (*nefesh* and *neshama).* The text reads: "The Source formed the human from the dust of the earth, blowing into the human's nostrils the breath of life *(nishmat chaim):* and then, the human became a living being/ soul (*nefesh*)." And later, in Exodus 31:16-17, we read, "The Israelite people will keep Shabbat, observing Shabbat throughout the ages as a covenant for all time, it will be a sign for all time between Me and the people of Israel. For in six days the Divine made heaven and earth, and on the seventh day, ceased from work and was refreshed (*va-yinafash).*

Our aliveness depends on our capacity to pause, breathe, rest, and refresh our souls. When we ignore this need, we suffer. When we lose this capacity, we cease to exist. When we choose to rest and breathe, we experience freedom in the present moment, especially when we feel the weight of anti-Jewish oppression in our bodies and lives. To simply rest, breathe, and refresh is a radical teaching, because—everyone—all human beings, all living beings, and even the Divine, need to pause, breathe, and rest to thrive. The *Sefer HaBahir* (the Book of Brightness), a thirteenth century kabbalistic text teaches, "What is Shabbat compared to? It is like a fountain in the midst of a garden: when the fountain flows, the entire garden flourishes."[46] Shabbat gives us the framework: we are worthy and deserving of rest, not because we have earned it or proved our worthiness as Jews, but simply because we are alive in this difficult world.

This recognition of the need for rest also forms a central aspect of the Ten Teachings, first in Exodus 20, where we're instructed to remember Shabbat and keep it sacred (*zachor et yom ha-Shabbat l'kadsho* in Hebrew), and then reiterated in Deuteronomy 5, where we're instructed to observe Shabbat and keep it sacred (*shamor et yom ha-Shabbat l'kadsho).* Remembering and observing our fundamental need for rest is a sacred *mitzvah* – an act of care for ourselves. But what is the difference between remembering to rest and observing rest? Rabbeinu Bahya, a fourteenth century Spanish rabbi, writes:

> *Zachor* [remember] is the attribute of compassion, and *shamor* [observe] is the attribute of justice. This was why there were two tablets [of the Ten Teachings], one tablet corresponding to the attribute of compassion and the second tablet, on which there also five statements, corresponding to the attribute of justice.

Pausing to remember to rest and breathe reflects compassion for ourselves. Observing our need to rest, by taking a break from incessant grinding and oppressive stress, points toward a more just world—a world where we collectively honor our bodies and our souls. This glimpse of compassion and justice from fourteenth century Jewish Spain before the Inquisition and expulsion resonates differently now, in the oppressive climate of twenty-first century in the U.S.

Trisha Hershey, founder of the Nap Ministry and author of *Rest is Resistance: A Manifesto,* argues that making space for rest is a form of radical healing, liberation from racial (and other forms of) oppression, social change, redemption, and collective care.[47] When we choose to pause, breathe, and rest our nervous system, we are reclaiming our dignity and power. We are choosing to privilege our emotional and physical safety over internalized anti-Jewish contempt. Pause and breathe flips our scripts of Jewish anxiety and shame to center our own well-being instead of trying to prove we are worthy of care and acceptance to others. This is a powerful practice.

I wish I had taken to heart the practice of pause and breathe earlier in my life. For twenty-five years, from the time I began graduate school to mid-way through rabbinical school, I engaged in some serious overwork-striver-perfectionism patterns. Before rabbinical school, I worked full-time, parented my daughter, and had various side hustle projects in the Jewish non-profit space. I rarely, if ever took a full day off to rest. Even though I technically remembered and observed Shabbat with Friday night blessings and a meal, and often went to synagogue on Shabbat morning, I didn't really *get it* spiritually, about the gift of pause, breathe, and rest. I would blow off my body's clear need to nap on Shabbat afternoon. Instead, I would try to cram a week's worth of reading for my rabbinical school classes on Sundays. I deluded myself that this was what productivity, virtue, and success looked like. I seriously ignored my body's cues and paid a terrible price: chronic fatigue, stress, inflammation, and a diagnosis of multiple sclerosis. I now recognize, with compassion and kindfulness, how my overwork habits were distraction and avoidance anxiety about worthiness, acceptance, and belonging.

Thankfully, the more I have leaned into pause, breathe, rest, and refresh, the more my anxiety has diminished over the years. Taking a Shabbat pause to pause, breathe, and simply *be* is a much more rewarding alternative to the anxiety of feeling like I needed to be *doing something.* Now, when I notice my jaw is clenched, or my shoulders are creeping up toward my ears, or when I have the urge to fidget with my hands or shred my cuticles (all signs of discomfort, tension, constriction, and anxiety), I compassionately deploy the kindful practice of pause and breathe, to rest and refresh my nervous system. When I realize I feel triggered or anxious, I stop what I'm doing, instinctively put my hand on my heart and inhale deeply to be with compassion for my own suffering and humanity. All it takes is ninety seconds of pausing to rest and breathe, to notice a change.

This breathing practice, described as a ninety-second reset, has been used in various spiritual traditions. The practice involves a regularly paced inhale, followed by a longer exhale, repeating a few times, and then moving into slower, deeper breaths for the remaining minute. You can try it now and observe what happens in your body and your mind, and you don't even need to close your eyes (but I find that closing my eyes helps to settle my nervous system down). You might notice that your shoulders and facial muscles relax. You might notice a calm settling of your body. It's a powerful practice you can deploy any time you notice that you're feeling anxious because it's so simple: pause and breathe.

When I teach this, some of my students ask worried what-if questions. "What if I pause and breathe 100 times a day, and I don't get my work done?" "What if I pause and breathe, and someone makes fun of me?" "What if I pause and breathe, and nothing changes?" If you're feeling worried right now about all the times you might pause and breathe over the course of your day, and fear that this practice might get in the way of your productivity, I want to offer you some reassurance and perspective.

Feeling anxious and tying that to our productivity, success, and worth is not helpful. It's a thought distortion, encouraged by our economic system. We're not productive, successful, and worthy because we're anxious. We might be productive *despite* feeling anxious all the time. (Side note: maybe if we were less pre-occupied with, and worried about, productivity and success, we might feel less anxious.) Noticing that we're anxious and pausing to breathe with kindfulness and compassion is a better alternative that can enable you to focus more fully from moment to moment, rather than anxiously doing something, multitasking, feeling agitated, stressed out all the time.

I've often asked my students a few what-if questions in reverse. What is the best thing that could happen if you paused to simply rest and breathe when you're anxious? What's the best thing that could happen if you simply breathed into that experience of anxiety with kindful compassion? What if you just gave it a try for a day, a week, or a month, and notice what happens? We just might settle ourselves down and feel the rewards of pause and breathe as a sacred mitzvah of rest.

Here's an invitation to practice pause and breathe with kindful compassion: over the next hour, simply notice your breathing. When you observe that your breathing is shallow or rapid, that you're holding your breath, or you've forgotten to breathe because you're anxious, just take a Shabbat pause. Notice what happens when you pause to observe your breath—do you immediately jump into anxious thoughts about the next thing on your to-do list? Do you feel too pressured to get going rather than focus on your breath? Simply observe with kindness and compassion the flow of sensations, thoughts and feelings. Perhaps you might notice that your breathing changes over that minute of pause. You can repeat this pause and breathe practice as many times as you want over an hour, a day, a month, a year, a lifetime.

THE SHEMA AND LISTENING TO THE BREATH OF BEING AND BECOMING

שְׁמַע יִשְׂרָאֵל יְהוָה אֱלֹהֵינוּ יְהוָה אֶחָד׃

Shema Yisrael Havaya Eloheinu Havaya Echad.

> Listen (pay attention), people who struggle with Being. Being is our Source, and Being is Oneness. (Deuteronomy 6:4)

Another unlearning practice is to listen. What I mean here is not just hearing but listening as a spiritual practice, to remember our interconnection: our relationship with our breath, bodies, and our aliveness; our relationship with ourselves and other human beings (across all our myriad differences); our relationship with all living beings on our shared planet; our relationship with our place in the cosmos.

Listening deeply to our breath and our bodies is a way to pay attention to what's happening in the present moment to remember that we are never alone, that we're part of something larger that connects us all to one another. Listening deeply, particularly to our breathing, is a powerful alternative when we get activated into the Four F's. Listening to our breathing when we realize we're activated can pull us out of ruminating about the past or anxiously worrying about the future. To unpack listening as a Jewish discernment practice, let's explore a text from Torah that many of us encounter in Jewish prayer: the *Shema.*

Here's some context about where the *Shema* comes from. In Deuteronomy, the last book of the Torah, Moses receives and then gives over some important instructions to the formerly enslaved Israelites, who are eager to end their forty years of wandering in the desert and cross the Jordan River. The *Shema,* one of the most famous sentences in Deuteronomy chapter 6 has become a central piece of Jewish liturgy for over two millennia. Jews sing or chant the *Shema* in daily services, at *Neilah* (the concluding service at the end of Yom Kippur), and for some Jews, it's the last prayer spoken or offered in *Vidui,* the set of prayers offered when a person transitions toward death.

You might be familiar with a classic, nineteenth-century translation of the *Shema*: "Hear O Israel, Adonai is Our God, Adonai is One." Truthfully, I cringe when I see this translation. The archaic language misses an opportunity to access the deep wisdom of the text. I translate the *Shema* differently, with the hope that you can connect with the potential for kindful compassion hidden within it. This is why my translation is:

> Listen (pay attention), people who struggle with Being.
> Being is our Source, and Being is Oneness.

I'd like to briefly explore each word to unpack the possibilities for unlearning.

Pay Attention

The root of the word *Shema* means to listen or to hear. I prefer listen or pay attention, because these verbs, given in the command form in Hebrew, imply our agency and choice. Listening requires awareness, connection, and conscious observation. Have you ever talked with someone and sensed that they're not really paying attention? They might be distracted, checked out, having their own internal churning thoughts, or if you're in an argument, they're judging and rehearsing what they're going to say next to bolster their own position. They might hear what you're saying but not deeply listening.

Like many people in aging bodies, I'm beginning to struggle with some hearing loss, especially in public spaces where there's lots of ambient noise. However, my changing ability to hear does not diminish my capacity to fully listen, pay attention, and be present. In fact, listening is essential to my job as a rabbi. Every day, I listen and pay attention to the music, the pain, and the unspoken longings underneath people's words. When people vulnerably share what's happening in their lives, one of their deepest, unspoken needs is to be listened to—feel heard and seen. Listening in this way demands my undivided, non-judgmental, non-anxious, and loving attention. As I get older, I consciously choose to practice kindful, compassionate listening: to my family, to the people I serve and to the inner wisdom of my body. In these difficult times of war and political polarization, I choose kindful, compassionate listening to pay attention to the humanity of others, especially people with whom I vigorously disagree.

Learning to kindfully, compassionately listen to what we might need from moment-to-moment can also help us re-center when we're anxious. We can better pay attention to the range of choices available to us. When we feel afraid or uncertain, instead of catastrophizing and asking ourselves what's the worst thing that might happen, we can build on our Shabbat pause and breathe. We can listen to what our nervous system is signaling to us and discern what we need.

Yisrael

This word commonly refers to the people of Israel, or Jews. It's important to understand the context for *Yisrael*, because it connects to the next word in the *Shema,* which is an unpronounceable name for the Divine.

The first mention of the word occurs in Genesis 32. In this chapter, Jacob is about to re-encounter his brother Esau, after many years of estrangement. Years earlier Jacob pretends to be Esau, the first-born son, and asks his dying father Isaac to give him a birthright blessing. When Esau discovers the ruse, he understandably feels betrayed and angry. Jacob flees from Esau's rage, builds a new life and amasses wealth. He's returning home. The day before this reunion with Esau, fearing the worst, Jacob strategically sends his family and flocks ahead of him. He spends the night alone. A mysterious messenger appears, and they wrestle all night. The messenger injures Jacob's hip socket as they struggle, and as the first glimmer of the sun appears, Jacob demands a blessing from this stranger. The messenger says, "Your name will no longer be Jacob, but *Israel*, for you have struggled with beings divine and human, and have prevailed."

I have always read this narrative as an allegory for wrestling with one's conscience after causing harm. Jacob's wrestling all night illuminates the transformation, indeed, the blessings, that emerge when we do the spiritual work to repair our relationships with ourselves and with others, *especially* when we've caused harm.

Who among us hasn't struggled at some point in our lives? We all struggle with feeling safe enough, loved enough, worthy enough, and accepted. Struggle, whether in relationship with self, people or the Divine, is a basic aspect of our aliveness. Remembering that it's human to struggle helps us feel less alone. Instead of cycling through our worry and shame habits, we can offer kindful compassion to ourselves. We can pause, rest, breathe, and remember our agency in those painful moments. We can prevail and keep moving forward in our lives, *despite* the difficulties.

YHVH/Havayah: Being and Becoming

> *My spirituality says YHVH, and me and my anxiety are one. I think anxiety points the finger at where unification and healing need to happen. The thing that I see is other than myself or something unwanted that I'm pushing away—that's not me. But what I need to learn what to say is yes, this is me, and accept it and understand the blessing of this anxiety. You touch the blessings in the mezuzah, punctuated by moments of remembering the Divine, pulling us out of our small self throughout the day. I think that's the antidote.*
>
> **—Y, sixties**

The next Hebrew word in the Shema is YHVH, which no one knows how to pronounce. In Greek, this word is also called the Tetragrammaton, or the four letters. You might have noticed that I do not translate word יְהוָה or YHVH in English as "Adonai," which means "my Lord."

All the metaphors we use, like Adonai, Elohim (plural for they/them), the Divine, King of the Universe, Source, God, HaShem (the Name) constrain our experience by the limits of language. We use metaphor to describe an experience of something ultimately ineffable, something we experience when we feel expansive, spacious, connected, loved, deeply moved and/or changed. But that something is beyond cognition, intellect, or conceptual framework. YHVH is one way our ancestors tried to describe that experience of the ineffable. One of my teachers, Rabbi Zalman Schachter-Shalomi, taught: "Theology is the afterthought of spiritual experience, not the other way around.

We are not trying to construct some top-down authoritative system, but to nourish the seeds of our own personal spiritual experience. We start with wonder, or with thankfulness, or yearning, or even rage, and we ask ourselves: Wonder or rage at what? Thankfulness toward what? Yearning for what? It was simple, searching questions like these that started our ancestors thinking in terms of 'God.'"[48]

The letters of this unpronounceable name evoke the Hebrew verb tense "to be," as in "what was *(hayah),* what is *(hoveh),* and will be *(yihiyeh).*" These Hebrew letters, re-arranged in different ways, all point to the idea of existence in time. Rabbi Arthur Green, a renowned scholar of Hasidism, simply translates this four-letter word as Being *(Havayah* in Hebrew). Drawing on his deep immersion in classic Jewish mystical texts, he writes: "When I refer to 'God,' I mean the inner force of existence itself, that of which one might say: 'Being is.' To speak of Being as a religious person, however, is to speak of it not detachedly, in 'scientific objectivity,' but rather with full engagement of the self, in love and awe."[49]

Being has no gender and does not evoke personhood, unlike the anthropomorphic metaphors King *(melech)* or my lord *(Adonai).* Being suggests existence as an unfolding process through time, rather than something static, unchanging, up there in the sky or outside us. Being is both transcendent and immanent—beyond us and within us. As Genesis 2 reminds us, we are all breathed into being, and breathing is what connects us to everything else that is alive. And when we die, we become something else, something mysterious, something that is still connected to Being, even though it remains a mystery.

Being, consciousness, existence or aliveness, is something we can reconnect with at any point in our day when we pause, breathe, listen, and pay attention. We don't need to *believe* in being: we experience it. We have consciousness that we are alive, we are aware of our breathing and *being.*

HAVAYA (BEING) FIVE FINGER BREATHING PRACTICE

Here is a calming practice that involves pause, breath, sight, and touch, and enlists the idea/experience of *Havayah*—Being. I call this the *Havaya* (Being) five finger breathing practice. I learned this as a secular, multisensory practice from Dr. Jud Brewer, and adapted the form as a Jewish practice using the ideas described above in the *Shema.* This simple practice can pull you out of a habit loop when you're experiencing racing thoughts and/or breathing and put you back into your body in less than ninety seconds.

Take one hand in front of you and spread your fingers out comfortably. It doesn't matter which hand you use. Then take the index finger of your other hand, and gently place it on your wrist, below your thumb. Make an audible inhale (not huge, just a regular breath), which sounds like "ha" as you trace your thumb with your finger to the top. When you get to the top of your thumb, softly say "va" and on the exhale down your thumb, make an audible "yah." Inhale "ha" up to the top of your index finger, "va" at the top, and "yah" on the way down. What you're literally saying is Being while listening to your Being as you inhale and exhale your breath.

I typically practice listening to my breath, using my index finger to trace my other fingers all the way to my wrist below my pinky finger, and then reverse direction until my index finger is back to my wrist under my thumb. You can also practice this breathing with your eyes closed if you want to pay more attention to the senses of touch and listening, without sight.

My breathing always changes and slows down when I deploy this practice, usually by the time I reach my ring finger on the first go-around. I've also noticed that the combination of listening to my saying "*Havaya*" as I inhale, and exhale redirects my attention away from thoughts about the past or future and puts me squarely into the present moment of sensation. Sometimes it feels more powerful to close my eyes while I breathe and trace my hand. I encourage you to experiment with this practice and see what works for you.

Eloheinu

This next word in the *Shema* is *Eloheinu*, or Being is ours, but not in any sense of Jewish separation, particularism, ownership, superiority, or domination. My interpretation of *Eloheinu* is staunchly universalist, to connect our Being, our aliveness and breath to every other living and breathing being on this planet.

I see *Eloheinu* as an invitation to remember that being and aliveness transcends differences among humans, animals, and plants, and that the entire, pulsing, breathing, interconnected web of life is infused with Being. This interconnection of being continues to unfold, no matter how alienated, polarized, or estranged we are from one another. Interconnection underlies everything that is alive, no matter how much people abuse their power, make terrible decisions that cause suffering, or pollute our planet. Being connects us all, always.

This framing of *Eloheinu* helps me when I get stressed out, angry, or scared by reading the news, and when I'm feeling Jewishly anxious. *Eloheinu,* remembering that we're all connected, reminds me to re-center myself and remember the humanity of others, when I feel scared or hurt and want to fight, lash out, and seek revenge. *Eloheinu* reminds me of the Jewish concept of *b'tzelem Elohim*, first described in Genesis 1. We are all created in the image of Being, and Being is plural, just like the Hebrew word *Elohim. Eloheinu,* Being is all of ours, forms the bedrock of my commitment to practicing non-violent speech and action, even in these politically difficult times. This reminder, that Being is all of ours, points to the very last word in the *Shema*.

Echad

The classic translation of *echad* is one. I translate it in the noun form, as oneness, which suggests wholeness. A simple way to understand oneness begins at the individual level: to remember that we're already whole and worthy of love, care, acceptance, and belonging. We are enough Jewishly and in all the other identities we hold. There's nothing we need to change about ourselves, and we are part of something bigger than just us. We can simply *be* and rest in the idea of Oneness to connect to our own wholeness. This idea of Oneness/wholeness has brought me great comfort when I have felt scared, unworthy, or scared that I might be rejected or excluded because of who I am as a Jew.

Another specifically Jewish way to think about Oneness is communal, and I often remind myself of an Aramaic phrase that comes from Talmud, Shevuot 39a: "*Kol Yisrael aravim zeh bazeh.*" This means, "All the people who struggle with the Divine are responsible for one another." Not only am *I* whole already, but *all of us Jews* (and our allies and beloveds) are whole, and part of my community, including and transcending our myriad differences. We can presume that loving intention to lean on one another when we're feeling scared, vulnerable, lonely, unsure of our worthiness, or questioning whether we belong.

Oneness also points to an even broader interconnection that transcends Jewish particularity: all living beings are connected, beyond our differences, disagreements, conflicts, inequalities, stratifications, and violence against one another. To remember Oneness is to expand our consciousness beyond the ways we human beings divide ourselves and cause pain with one another, beyond the connections we can readily see and understand. We can remember that we are but a tiny speck of aliveness, part of a vast, greater Oneness in the universe.

This remembering Oneness helps to pull me out of my well-grooved, habitual thoughts and feelings (of fear, inadequacy, reactivity, taking things personally, presuming exclusion, etc.) into a wider, more expansive perspective. To strengthen this expansion habit, I keep a postcard of Pandora's Cluster (four billion light years from Earth) near my laptop when I'm working and need a break. When I feel stressed out or anxious, I often find solace and wonder in the astonishing photos from the Hubble space telescope. When I look at Hubble photos of galaxies far beyond ours, I remember that all the cosmic dust, gases, electrons, protons, and neutrons that create such beauty in the universe also reside inside me, in everyone I love, in every living being on the planet.

I also think about the overview effect from space, which turns my awe into feeling tenderness towards other people, plants, trees, and the earth. The overview effect, coined in the 1980s by author Frank White, describes a cognitive, emotional, and spiritual shift that astronauts have experienced when viewing the earth from space. When astronauts look at Earth, tiny in comparison to the vastness of space, they see everyone and everything they love from a distance. In those moments, astronauts have reported feeling a sense of awe, wonder, curiosity, peace, and self-transcendence. It shifts perspective by demonstrating that everything on planet Earth is interconnected. This is a wonderful paradox! By getting some distance from the tangle of our thoughts and feelings (especially anxiety!), we can begin to see more clearly and expansively. By cultivating distance, we can experience a different perspective on what's happening and not get sucked into the immediacy and intensity of whatever might be triggering us. Have you ever visited a place (most likely in nature) that simply bowled you over with awe, wonder, and curiosity? Those kinds of feelings—of both spaciousness and interconnection are an example of the overview effect, or an experience of Oneness.

In Jewish mystical tradition there's a teaching that we constantly move between two states of consciousness, like an infinity circle.

One state of mind is *mochin d'katnut,* which means constricted mind or "small consciousness." If you have ever heard of the Hebrew word *katan* (small or little), *katnut* is the noun form. I think of *mochin d'katnut* as a helpful state of mind that we use to get stuff done in life: chores around the house, tasks, lists, projects, grocery shopping, laundry, etc. It's our everyday consciousness that enables us to function in the world.

But *Mochin d'katnut* can also be a space we live in when we're feeling anxious. It's the headspace of "what if the worst thing happens," when our vision and bodies become constricted with fear, uncertainty, and anxiety. When we're inside an anxiety habit loop, running on a familiar hamster wheel of judgmental, critical thoughts and feelings about ourselves and others, we're in *mochin d'katnut.*

Mochin d'gadlut means "big mind" or expanded consciousness, or remembering Oneness, from the Hebrew word for big, *gadol.* I associate this state of being in our minds and bodies with spaciousness, openness, and compassion. We can reconnect with *mochin d'gadlut* and that sense of interconnected Oneness anywhere, anytime, *especially* as a better alternative to our anxiety habits. How do we do this? We can simply pause to notice, give our nervous systems a rest, breathe deeply, zoom out, and remember that we're part of something much larger to get in touch with *mochin d'gadlut,* expansive mind.

WITNESSING IN THE SHEMA AND WITNESSING OURSELVES

When the *Shema* is written in Hebrew, two of the letters are larger than the others. In the first word, the *ayin* or ע, which has no sound by itself, is enlarged. And in the very last word, *echad* (one or oneness), the *dalet* or ד is bigger. This is deliberate: it's how the *Shema* is written in the Torah. In Hebrew, these two letters, when placed next to one another form the word *eyd* עד, which means two different things: until, to exist, and witness, in the noun form. I find the idea of witness most compelling here. The *Shema* is an invitation to witness ourselves, other living beings, and all of creation, from the standpoint of loving, compassionate Presence. What does witness mean in this context?

I think the key to our unlearning is to practice being a compassionate witness to what arises in our lives from moment to moment. We can witness what's happening in our bodies and our breath, as a powerful way to create distance from our anxiety habit loops, like the overview effect. We can practice witnessing our suffering with kindfulness, rather than judgment, harshness, or shame. We can simply pause to witness and *be with* our experience in all its fullness: the sensations, the feelings, the thoughts—without trying to change or do anything. Through Jewish practices of pause, breathe, listen, and witness, we can create some space to discern what we need when we're feeling triggered, scared, stressed out, and anxious, and make different choices than what we usually reach for. We can witness and remember that we're part of something larger. We can turn towards the joy we deserve, not because we've earned or proved it, but simply because we exist, we are part of Being itself.

Chapter 6

ALEINU: IT'S UP TO US

It is upon us to comfort the sick in body and heart.
It is upon us to bring joy to those around us.
It is upon us to face the truth, no matter how difficult.
It is upon us to see that justice is done, which is not always easy.
It is upon us to know when we have choices, and to make them.
It is upon us to be mindful and to notice what we see with compassion.
We are all one in the One-ness, there is no other.

—Trisha Arlin[50]

I began writing this book with the concept of *tikkun atzmi*: how we can heal ourselves from the anxiety generated by anti-Jewish contempt. So many Jews care deeply about healing the world—*tikkun olam*, but many of us bypass or avoid the necessary work of looking inward, to heal ourselves of the pain we carry. Healing ourselves and the world are interdependent, like braided strands in a challah.

Aleinu: it's up to us to heal ourselves of our anxiety habits around safety, worth, acceptance, and belonging. It's up to us to face difficult truths about our anxiety habits that amplify our suffering. It's up to us to recognize we have choices and to practice kindfulness and compassion for ourselves. It's up to us to pause, breathe, listen, and discern what we *really* need so that we can make choices to support our nervous systems. I hope that you have found resources, concepts, and practices in this book to help you begin to take responsibility for your own healing from anti-Jewish oppression—both the external difficulties we face in this challenging world, and those which we internalize.

This book begins and ends with the same questions. What would your life feel like if you felt less anxious all the time? How would it feel to experience more joy? Now that you have more insights and answers, perhaps you can widen your communal lens to look at the world.

What might life look like for all of us Jews if we lived with less internalized anti-Jewish oppression? How might moving away from fear, uncertainty, and anxiety habits free up more space in our heads, our bodies, and our lives? What would it look like if we collectively moved through the world feeling freer, more expansive, more open, and more connected to our bodies and our needs? How might you and I, and all of us, spend our time and resources differently? What might we creatively envision and accomplish together, with our allies and partners beyond the Jewish world? How might this collective unlearning process change the world to create more compassion and justice?

My life has changed substantially, for the better, through unlearning my Jewish anxiety habits. I no longer suffer from insomnia, nor imposter syndrome. I no longer harshly judge or criticize the shape or size of my body. I no longer automatically catastrophize and assume the worst will happen. I no longer anxiously doomscroll. I have chosen instead to set aside more time to rest, pause, breathe, listen to my body, hug trees as a gratitude practice, practice kindful compassion, make art, sing in a feminist chorus, and participate in local social justice efforts. I have unlearned my writing anxiety to finish this book.

I believe, with all my heart, and all my soul, that we are entitled to joy. Not because we have earned it, but simply because we are alive in this world. We are worthy and deserving to live with freedom from crippling Jewish anxiety. We are entitled to make choices about how to respond to an uncertain world with awareness, curiosity, compassion, and courage—for ourselves, and in relationships with our beloveds, friends, and allies. Freedom, liberation, and joy are our birthrights. This is a radical claim in a world that seeks to diminish and oppress us through harm, contempt, disgust, and revulsion.

The most powerful form of resistance to that anti-Jewish oppression is to insist on our inherent dignity, worth, and belonging in this world. Yes, it is difficult to be a Jew in a broken world. We get to choose whether we live in fear that constricts our lives and our capacity for joy. We can unlearn our anxiety habits and choose better alternatives to celebrate our aliveness. We can be kind and compassionate with ourselves. We can pause, rest, breathe, listen, dance, sing, make art, and organize for change, *despite* our inherited trauma, despite the deep and unfolding pain of the world, despite the real oppression and contempt that characterize the world we live in. Pausing to rest, breathe, listen, and play, especially when our hearts are weary are acts of resistance to oppression and contempt.

We can respond to Jewish anxiety triggers with deeper awareness of our choices about how to respond. We can resource ourselves with different strategies and better alternatives to the previous habits that amplified and increased our anxiety. We can recognize how the past haunts the present and *still choose* to nourish ourselves through pausing to breathe, re-center our bodies, and discern our response. We can grow our awareness, curiosity, compassion and courage. AND: we can also step into more power, more compassion, and more kindfulness, without catastrophizing, contracting, or collapsing into fear.

This is the braided challah of *tikkun atzmi* and *tikkun olam*—healing ourselves and harnessing our insights and energy to heal the world. When we transform our anxiety habits, we transform our lives and those around us. Our individual transformation can then ripple out into the wider world in how we respond to fear, uncertainty and oppression. When we work together to heal our Jewish anxiety and internalized oppression, we can envision and build a different world. We can respond to the anti-Jewish oppression that exists in the world from a more grounded, embodied, and calmer place to soften, dissolve, and disarm that oppression.

And, *lo aleinu:* it's not only our responsibility. It's not only up to us to soften and dissolve anti-Jewish contempt and oppression. This is the responsibility and work of our allies and partners in justice movements who care about Jewish safety, respect, acceptance, and belonging. When we are well-resourced, we can enlist our partners and allies to help us stay safe. We can invite our allies to do the reparative work of changing hearts and minds in their own communities to soften and dissolve anti-Jewish contempt, ignorance, and oppression. We can work across other communities that experience oppression to build a better, kinder, more compassionate, more just world for all of us. It's time.

ACKNOWLEDGMENTS

Thank you to Jo Kent Katz and Cherie Brown for paving the way with transcendingjewish trauma.com.

To Trisha Arlin, for permission to use her poem, "Aleinu."

Thank you to Aly Halpert, for permission to open this book with "Loosen."

To Merle Feld, for permission to use the poem, "Dreaming of Home."

To Rabbi Dr. Tirzah Firestone and Dr. Jud Brewer: your leadership helped me to have the courage to add my voice to this unfolding conversation about trauma, habits, anxiety, and healing.

My deep gratitude to Anne Pogoriler and Nancy Wadsworth, for sitting on my front porch to listen to my initial, inchoate ideas, and for reading a draft of Chapter 3.

To my students: you continue to teach and inspire me.

To all the wonderful people who agreed to be interviewed for this book: thank you for your candor and vulnerability.

Thank you to Rabbi Miriam Margles of the Institute for Jewish Spirituality for your collegial support, companionship, and spiritual leadership in this emerging field.

To Rabbi Brian Field, for your many years of rabbinic mentorship.

To Jon Sweeney and the Monkfish team for taking a chance on this book and making it better.

To sefaria.org for the amazing online Jewish library from where many Jewish textual sources in this book came.

To friends and colleagues who listened and offered insights: Shayndel Adler, Jeremy Anderson, Esther Azar, Rachel Balows, Diana Brewer, Marian Brown, Ken Brown, Sarah Rosenberg Brown, Sarah Burgamy, Robin Chalecki, Shari Edelstein, Karen Erlichman, Bonnie Feinberg, Lievnath Faber, Amanda Glaser, Jenny Glick, Melanie Gruenwald, Salomon Gruenwald, Steven Gottlieb, Tamara Hale, Meg Hogan, Andrea Jacobs, Miriam Kapner, Bex Kagan, Irwin Keller, Sarah Kornhauser, Matthew LeBauer, Jessica Kessler Marshall, T.J. Michels, Sara Nadelman, Amy Grossblatt Pessah, Jamie Polliard, Jessi Roemer, Josh Rolnick, Danya Ruttenberg, Stephanie Rudnick, Jamie Sarche, Jennifer Sarche, Laura Saunders, Sarah Shapiro-Plevan, Anna Sher, Eran Shlomi, Fran Simon, Whitney Weathers, Ken Weil, Elsbeth Williams, Dave Yedid, and Erin Yourtz. If I've forgotten to thank anyone, I ask for your forgiveness and grace.

Thank you to the staff and board at Judaism Your Way. You offered encouragement, support, a sabbatical, and the space to develop, teach, and write these ideas into being. A deep bow of gratitude and appreciation for each of you.

To my family, Carol, Chuck, my aunt Anita, my sister, Amy Abrams and the Brooklyn crew: thank you. You watched this book evolve and supported me every step of the way. I am grateful.

To Sasha and Dawnie: for everything, with love.

REFERENCES

All Jewish textual sources referenced can be found at www.sefaria.org.

Trisha Arlin, *Place Yourself: Words of Prayer & Intention* (Dimus Parhessia Press, 2022).

Baron, Salo W., "Newer Emphases in Jewish History," *Jewish Social Studies 25* no. 4 (1963): 245–58.

Peter Beinart, *Being Jewish After the Destruction of Gaza: A Reckoning* (Knopf, 2025).

David Biale, ed. *Cultures of the Jews: A New History* (Schocken, 2012).

Eugene B. Borowitz, *Choices in Modern Jewish Thought: A Partisan Guide* (Berhman House, 1983).

Ajahn Brahm, *Kindfulness* (Wisdom Publications, 2016).

Judson Brewer, *Unwinding Anxiety: New Science Shows How to Break the Cycles of Worry and Fear to Heal Your Mind* (Avery, 2022).

Charles Duhigg, *The Power of Habit: Why We Do What We Do in Life and Business* (Random House, 2014).

Merle Feld, *Finding Words* (Behrman House, 2011).

Diane Fersko, *We Need to Talk About Antisemitism* (Seal Press, 2023).

Tirzah Firestone, *Wounds into Wisdom: Healing Intergenerational Jewish Trauma* (Monkfish Book Publishing, 2019).

Franklin Foer, "The Golden Age of American Jews is Ending," *Atlantic Monthly,* April 2024.

B.J. Fogg, *Tiny Habits: The Small Changes that Change Everything* (Harvest, 2019).

Goldberg, S.B., Tucker, R.P., Greene, P.A., Davidson, R.J., Wampold, B.E., Kearney, D.J., and Simpson, T.L. "Mindfulness-based interventions for psychiatric disorders: A systematic review and meta-analysis" (2018). *Clinical Psychology Review, 59,* 52–60.

Eric L. Goldstein, *The Price of Whiteness: Jews, Race, and American Identity* (Princeton University Press, 2008).

Arthur Green, *Radical Judaism: Rethinking God and Tradition* (Yale University Press, 2010).

Jesse Green, "Let Us Tell You a Story: How Jewish People Built the American Theater as We Know It," *New York Times Magazine,* November 29, 2023.

Ronnie Grinberg, *Write Like a Man: Jewish Masculinity and the New York Intellectuals* (Princeton University Press, 2024).

Prentiss Hemphill, *What It Takes to Heal: How Transforming Ourselves Can Change the World* (Random House, 2024).

Judith L. Herman, *Trauma and Recovery: The Aftermath of Violence, From Domestic Abuse to Political Terror* (Basic Books, 2015).

Trisha Hershey, *Rest is Resistance: A Manifesto* (Little Brown Spark, 2022).

James Jacobson-Maisels, "Tikkun Olam, Tikkun Atzmi: Healing the Self, Healing the World," in *Tikkun Olam: Judaism, Humanism, and Transcendence* (Mesorah Matrix, 2015), 354.

Rosalinda R. Jimenez, et al, "Vicarious Trauma in Mental Health Care Providers," *Journal of Interprofessional Education and Practice,* Volume 24: September 2021, https://www.sciencedirect.com/science/article/abs/pii/S2405452621000380

Resmaa Menakem, *My Grandmother's Hands: Racialized Trauma and the Pathway to Mending Our Hearts and Bodies* (Central Recovery Press, 2017).

Kristin Neff and Shauna Shapiro, *The Science of Mindfulness and Self-Compassion: How to Build New Habits to Transform Your Life* (Sounds True, 2019).

Kristen Neff and Shauna Shapiro, *The Yin and Yang of Self-Compassion: Cultivating Kindness and Strength in the Face of Difficulty* (Sounds True, 2019).

Adrienne Rich," Split at the Root: An Essay on Jewish Identity," *Snapshots of a Daughter-in-Law* (W.W. Norton, 1967), 36-40.

April Rosenbloom, *The Past Didn't Go Anywhere: Making Resistance to Antisemitism Part of All of Our Movements,* pamphlet, 2007.

Marshall Rosenberg, *Non-Violent Communication: A Language of Life* (Puddledancer Press, Third Edition, 2015).

Jeff Roth, *Jewish Meditation Practices for Everyday Life* (Jewish Lights Publishing, 2015).

Toba Spitzer, *God is Here: Reimagining the Divine* (St. Martins Press, 2022).

https://www.transcendingjewishtrauma.com/unpackingtrauma

Bessel van der Kolk, *The Body Keeps the Score: Brain, Mind, and Body in the Healing of Trauma* (Penguin, 2014).

Pete Walker, *Complex PTSD: From Surviving to Thriving* (Azure Coyote Publishing, 2013), 12-13.

Isabel Wilkerson, *Caste: The Origins of Our Discontents* (Random House, 2020).

Rachel Yehuda and Amy Lehrner, "Intergenerational transmission of trauma effects: putative role of epigenetic mechanisms," *World Psychiatry* 2018, Sep. 7;17(3):243–257.

Moshe Zimmerman, *Wilhelm Marr: The Patriarch of Anti-Semitism* (Oxford University Press, 1987).

NOTES

1 Merle Feld, *Finding Words* (Behrman House, 2011).

2 Pirkei Avot 1:14, https://www.sefaria.org/Pirkei_Avot.1.15?lang=bi

3 I conducted 40 interviews on Zoom in 2024 with Jews who identified across the denominational spectrum, from secular to Modern Orthodox. All participants live in the United States. The youngest interview participant was twenty-eight, the oldest in their seventies. People identified as queer and straight, and mostly cisgender. Two participants were transgender. More women than men volunteered, and I suspect this is because men have been socialized to avoid discussing vulnerable feelings.

4 James Jacobson-Maisels, "Tikkun Olam, Tikkun Atzmi: Healing the Self, Healing the World," in *Tikkun Olam: Judaism, Humanism, and Transcendence* (Mesorah Matrix, 2015), 354.

5 Aleinu, *It is our obligation,* is a Jewish prayer recited at the end of three daily prayer services and in the middle of the Musaf service during Rosh Hashanah. Most scholars credit authorship to Rav, a third century Babylonian scholar.

6 Judson Brewer, *Unwinding Anxiety: New Science Shows How to Break the Cycles of Worry and Fear to Heal Your Mind* (Avery, 2022).

7 Moshe Zimmerman, *Wilhelm Marr: The Patriarch of Anti-Semitism* (Oxford University Press, 1987).

8 Pete Walker, *Complex PTSD: From Surviving to Thriving* (Azure Coyote Publishing, 2013), 12-13.

9 BJ Fogg, *Tiny Habits: The Small Changes that Change Everything* (Harvest, 2019).

10 Charles Duhigg, *The Power of Habit: Why We Do What We Do in Life and Business* (Random House, 2014).

11 Here, I'm drawing on the somatic anti-racism work of Resmaa Menakem, particularly *My Grandmother's Hands: Racialized Trauma and the Pathway to Mending Our Hearts and Bodies* (Central Recovery Press, 2017). Chapters 3 and 9 discuss the intergenerational, traumatic impact of learning to disassociate from our bodies.

12 See, for example Ronnie Grinberg's *Write Like a Man: Jewish Masculinity and the New York Intellectuals* (Princeton University Press, 2024).

13 For a helpful visualization of feelings, see https://feelingswheel.com/.

14 Marshall Rosenberg, *Non-Violent Communication: A Language of Life* (Puddledancer Press, Third Edition, 2015).

15 Kristen Neff and Shauna Shapiro, *The Yin and Yang of Self-Compassion: Cultivating Kindness and Strength in the Face of Difficulty* (Sounds True, 2019).

16 Jesse Green, "Let Us Tell You a Story: How Jewish People Built the American Theater as We Know It," *New York Times Magazine*, November 29, 2023.

17 Diane Fersko, *We Need to Talk About Antisemitism* (Seal Press, 2023).

18 Prentiss Hemphill, *What It Takes to Heal: How Transforming Ourselves Can Change the World* (Random House, 2024), 30.

19 Bessel van der Kolk, *The Body Keeps the Score: Brain, Mind, and Body in the Healing of Trauma* (Penguin, 2014).

20 Judith L. Herman, *Trauma and Recovery: The Aftermath of Violence, From Domestic Abuse to Political Terror,* (Basic Books, 2015).

21 Isabel Wilkerson, *Caste: The Origins of Our Discontents* (Random House, 2020).

22 Baron, Salo W., "Newer Emphases in Jewish History," Jewish Social Studies 25 no. 4 (1963): 245–58.

23 David Biale, ed. *Cultures of the Jews: A New History* (Schocken, 2012).

24 Rachel Yehuda and Amy Lehrner, *Intergenerational transmission of trauma effects: putative role of epigenetic mechanisms,* World Psychiatry 2018 Sep 7;17(3):243–257.

25 Tirzah Firestone, *Wounds into Wisdom: Healing Intergenerational Jewish Trauma* (Monkfish Book Publishing, 2019).

26 Peter Beinart, *Being Jewish After the Destruction of Gaza: A Reckoning* (Knopf, 2025).

27 Rosalinda R. Jimenez, et al, "Vicarious Trauma in Mental Health Care Providers," *Journal of Interprofessional Education and Practice,* Volume 24: September 2021, https://www.sciencedirect.com/science/article/abs/pii/S2405452621000380

28 https://brenebrown.com/articles/2013/01/15/shame-v-guilt/

29 https://www.transcendingjewishtrauma.com/unpackingtrauma

30 Eric L. Goldstein, *The Price of Whiteness: Jews, Race, and American Identity* (Princeton University Press, 2008).

31 Adrienne Rich," Split at the Root: An Essay on Jewish Identity," *Snapshots of a Daughter-in-Law* (W.W. Norton, 1967), 36-40.

32 April Rosenbloom, *The Past Didn't Go Anywhere: Making Resistance to Antisemitism Part of All of Our Movements,* 2007, archived: https://www.aprilrosenblum.com/_files/ugd/4dc342_10d68441b6c44ee0a12909a242074ca6.pdf

33 https://www.sefaria.org/Sanhedrin.37a.13?lang=bi

34 Franklin Foer, "The Golden Age of American Jews is Ending," *Atlantic Monthly,* April 2024. Archived at: https://www.theatlantic.com/magazine/archive/2024/04/us-anti-semitism-jewish-american-safety/677469/

35 Prentiss Hemphill, *What It Takes to Heal: How Transforming Ourselves Can Change the World* (Random House, 2024), 32.

36 https://www.sefaria.org/Genesis.1.26?lang=bi&with=Commentary%20ConnectionsList&lang2=en

37 https://www.sefaria.org/Pirkei_Avot.2.2?lang=en

38 See, for example, Chapter 12," Postmodern Judaism," in Eugene B. Borowitz, *Choices in Modern Jewish Thought: A Partisan Guide* (Berhman House, 1983), 283-312.

39 Toba Spitzer, *God is Here: Reimagining the Divine* (St. Martins Press, 2022).

40 https://www.jewishspirituality.org/get-started/the-gift-of-awareness-2024/

41 Ajahn Brahm, *Kindfulness* (Wisdom Publications, 2016).

42 Goldberg, S.B., Tucker, R.P., Greene, P.A., Davidson, R.J., Wampold, B.E., Kearney, D.J., and Simpson, T.L. "Mindfulness-based interventions for psychiatric disorders: A systematic review and meta-analysis" (2018). *Clinical Psychology Review*, *59,* 52-60.

43 https://www.sefaria.org/sheets/533645?lang=bi

44 Kristin Neff and Shauna Shapiro, *The Science of Mindfulness and Self-Compassion: How to Build New Habits to Transform Your Life* (Sounds True, 2019).

45 Jeff Roth, *Jewish Meditation Practices for Everyday Life* (Jewish Lights Publishing, 2015) 18.

46 Sefer HaBahir: https://www.sefaria.org/Sefer_HaBahir?tab=contents

47 Trisha Hershey, *Rest is Resistance: A Manifesto* (Little Brown Spark, 2022).

48 Zalman Schachter-Shalomi, accessed through https://www.sefaria.org/sheets/545037?lang=bi

49 Arthur Green, *Radical Judaism: Rethinking God and Tradition* (Yale University Press, 2010), 19.

50 Trisha Arlin, *Place Yourself: Words of Prayer & Intention* (Dimus Parhessia Press, 2022).

Caryn Aviv is the rabbinic and program director at Judaism Your Way in Denver, CO. She's a rabbi, recovering academic in sociology and Jewish studies, and (mostly) formerly anxious Jew. She creates spaces, stories, rituals, and practices that offer safety, healing, equity, compassion and justice for Jews and their loved ones and allies. As a professor and rabbi she's taught Jewish history and culture for two decades, and she now teaches the material in this book in workshops, at conferences, with congregations, and online in partnership with national Jewish organizations all over the US. She lives in Denver, CO.

We are

Monkfish Book Publishing

...an independent press publishing spiritual and literary books from a diverse range of perspectives. Genres include memoirs, wisdom literature, fiction, and scholarly works of thought. Monkfish books appeal to the seasoned or novice seeker as well as to the general public looking for reliable sources on spirituality. The readers we had in mind when we began Monkfish in 2002 were devoted spiritual seekers, the type whose passion for the spiritual quest would lead them to read across a dazzling array of traditions: Buddhist, Hindu, Jewish, Christian, Muslim, Native American and more. It has always been our intent to publish works of spiritual authenticity for the general public as well as the specialist and scholar.

Our books are available from booksellers everywhere.

Use this QR code to see recently published books:

Use this one to sign-up for our monthly newsletter:

www.ingramcontent.com/pod-product-compliance
Lightning Source LLC
Jackson TN
JSHW022116141225
95602JS00001B/1

* 9 7 8 1 9 6 6 6 0 8 1 1 0 *